ROCKWELL LECTURES

Rice University

Previously published books in
the Rockwell Lecture series

The Structure of Christian Ethics
Joseph Sittler

Religion and American Democracy
Roy F. Nichols

Biblical Thought and the Secular University
George Arthur Buttrick

Darwin and the Modern World View
John C. Greene

The Lost Image of Man
Julian N. Hartt

The Moral Issue in Statecraft: Twentieth-Century
Approaches and Problems
Kenneth W. Thompson

Archaeology, Historical Analogy, and Early Biblical Tradition
William F. Albright

ON NEW CREATION

On New Creation

B. D. NAPIER

LOUISIANA STATE UNIVERSITY PRESS

Baton Rouge

ISBN 0-8071-0524-4
Library of Congress Catalog Card Number 70-134553
Copyright © 1971 by Louisiana State University Press
All rights reserved
Manufactured in the United States of America
Printed by The Parthenon Press, Nashville, Tennessee
Designed by J. Barney McKee

*This book is dedicated
to colleagues in the ministry
in university and church
whose work and passion are essential to
the creation of a new history.*

FOREWORD

It was for me an exciting and rewarding week at Rice University. The Rockwell Lectures are delivered in the evening, in that chaste, exquisite little chapel, with a small cross-section of the whole community joined—townspeople, faculty, and students; an easy place to speak; a warm, sensitive, perceptive audience. And my own induction into Rice, my brief participation in the life of that University, was enhanced by my lecturing, following a formal dinner, in Baker College (with a vigorous discussion later in the evening in the Master's House); my residence in Lovett College; and by the opportunity to lecture for three mornings to as responsive audiences of students as I have ever had.

My gratitude continues for the quality of Rice's hospitality. I am especially indebted to my friend of long standing, Professor Niels Nielsen, who initiated the invitation; to my former colleague at Yale and associate of Baker College, Professor Charles Garside; the Masters of Baker and Lovett colleges; another former colleague (at Georgia), Professor John Rath; and literally scores of others who made the occasion of the 1969 Rockwell Lectures such a memorable week.

The three original Rockwell Lectures were also delivered, with little change, as the Westervelt Lectures during Austin Seminary's Midwinter Lectures in February, 1969. They were revised, and the number of lectures expanded to five, for Princeton Theological Seminary's Institute of Theology and Union (Richmond) Theological Seminary's School of Theology in the summer of 1970.

I cannot close this foreword without acknowledging my really incalculable indebtedness to my wife Joy, my best, sharpest, most alert, and most loving critic; and to the students of Stanford University, from whom I have gained far more than I have given.

CONTENTS

ON NEW CREATION

Chapter I

BIBLICAL FOREWORD

Yahweh rises from his judgment seat, he stands up to arraign his people. Yahweh calls to judgment the elders and princes of his people. "You are the ones who destroy the vineyards and conceal what you have stolen from the poor. By what right do you crush my people, and grind the faces of the poor?" (Isaiah 3:13–15, JB) *

Are you not the ones who should know what is right, you, enemies of good and friends of evil? When they have devoured the flesh of my people and torn off their skin and crushed their bones; when they have shredded them like flesh in a pot and like meat in a cauldron. . . . (Micah 3:1–3, JB)

[Thus says the Lord:] I hate and despise your feasts, I take no pleasure in your solemn festivals. . . . I reject your oblations, and refuse . . . your sacrifices. . . . Let me have no more of the din of your chanting, no more of your strumming on harps. But let justice flow like water, and integrity like an unfailing stream. (Amos 5:21–24, JB)

Are not you and the Cushites all the same to me? . . . Did not I, who brought Israel out of the land of Egypt, also bring the Philistines from Caphtor, and the Aramaeans from Kir? Now, my eyes are turned on the sinful kingdom, to wipe it off the face of the earth. (Amos 9:7–8, JB)

Hear the word of Yahweh, you rulers of Sodom; listen

* Unless otherwise indicated, quoted scripture is taken from the *Revised Standard Version* of the Bible. The initials JB and NEB indicate the *Jerusalem Bible* and the *New English Bible*, respectively.

3

to the command of our God, you people of Gomorrah. What are your endless sacrifices to me? . . . I am sick of [them]. . . . Bring me your worthless offerings no more. . . . New Moons, sabbaths, assemblies—[a contemporary Isaiah might say, Thanksgiving, Christmas, Easter, and the Fourth of July] I cannot endure [at one and the same time] festival and solemnity. . . . You may multiply your prayers, I shall not listen. Your hands are covered with blood, wash, make yourselves clean. Take your wrong-doing out of my sight. Cease to do evil. Learn to do good, search for justice, help the oppressed. . . . If you are willing to obey, you shall eat the good things of the earth. But if you persist in rebellion, the sword shall eat you instead. (Isaiah 1:10–20, JB)

[The prophet Hosea sees a direct analogy between his own relationship to an unfaithful woman, and the relationship of God to people. One is not always sure whether the speaker is Hosea or Yahweh.]

I will lead you back into the wilderness . . . there you will respond to me as you did when you were young, as you did when you came out of the land of Egypt. . . . When that day comes, I will make a treaty on your behalf with the wild animals . . . I will abolish the bow, the sword, and war from the land; and I will make you lie down in safety. I will betroth you to myself forever, betroth you with integrity and justice, with tenderness and love. In that day, says the Lord, I will answer the heavens, and they shall answer the earth; and the earth shall answer the grain and the wine and the oil . . . and I will say, You are my people; and you will say, Thou art my God. (Hosea 2:14–18, adapted)

Jesus says: "You have heard that it was said to the men of old, 'You shall not kill; and whoever kills shall be liable to judgment.' But I say to you that every one who is angry with his brother shall be liable to judgment; whoever insults his brother shall be liable to the council, and whoever says, 'You fool!' shall be liable to the hell of fire. . . .

"You have heard that it was said, 'You shall not commit adultery.' But I say to you that every one who looks at a woman lustfully has already committed adultery with her in his heart. . . .

"You have heard that it was said, 'You shall love your neighbor and hate your enemy.' But I say to you, Love your enemies and pray for those who persecute you, so that you may be sons of your Father who is in heaven; for he makes his sun rise on the evil and on the good, and sends rain on the just and on the unjust. For if you love those who love you, what reward have you? Do not even the tax collectors do the same? And if you salute only your brethren, what more are you doing than others? Do not even the Gentiles do the same? You, therefore, must be perfect, as your heavenly Father is perfect. . . .

"Think not that I have come to abolish the law and the prophets; I have come not to abolish them but to fulfill them. For truly, I say to you, till heaven and earth pass away, not an iota, not a dot, will pass from the law until all is accomplished. Whoever then relaxes one of the least of these commandments and teaches men so, shall be called least in the kingdom of heaven; but he who does them and teaches them shall be called great in the kingdom of heaven. For I tell you, unless your righteousness exceeds that of the scribes and Pharisees, you will never enter the kingdom of heaven." (Matt. 5:21–22, 27–28, 43–48, and 17–20)

[Jesus returns from the Mount of Transfiguration to

find a vocal crowd milling around his disciples. One from the crowd speaks.]

"Teacher, I brought my son to you, for he has a dumb spirit; and wherever it seizes him, it dashes him down; and he foams and grinds his teeth and becomes rigid; and I asked your disciples to cast it out, and they were not able."

"Bring him to me."

And Jesus asked his father, "How long has he had this?" And he said, "From childhood. And it has often cast him into the fire and into the water, to destroy him; but if you can do anything, have pity on us and help us." And Jesus said to him, "If you can! All things are possible to him who believes." Immediately the father of the child cried out and said, "I believe; help my unbelief!"

[Jesus] rebuked the unclean spirit, saying to it, "You dumb and deaf spirit, I command you, come out of him, and never enter him again." And after crying out and convulsing him terribly, it came out, and the boy was like a corpse; so that most of the crowd said, "He is dead." But Jesus took him by the hand and lifted him up, and he arose. . . . His disciples asked him privately, "Why could we not cast it out?" And he said to them, "This kind cannot be driven out by anything but prayer." (Mark 9:14–29)

A NEW HISTORY: *The Generations*

A few years ago John Fowles wrote an astonishing novel, *The Magus*, about the adventures of a young man named Nicholas. At the beginning of the story, as he starts out on what is to be a totally new life, Nicholas says: "It poured with rain the day I left. But I was filled with excitement, a strange exuberant sense of taking wing. I didn't know where I was going, but I knew what I needed. I needed a new land, a new race, a new language; and, although I couldn't have put it into words then, I needed a new mystery." [1]

Nicholas might have summed it all up by saying that he needed a new history.

God knows we do.

It is a question whether, living in the old history, we will survive even the decade of the 1980's. The early stories of Genesis remind us that we have from the beginning endured a human climate polluted by arrogance, by self- or group-adulation, by mutual violence, and by the corruption and perversion of the human spirit. Given the fabulous escalation of our destructive powers in this last split second of the old history and our now-critical contamination not only

---

[1] John Fowles, *The Magus* (Boston, Toronto: Little, Brown and Company, 1965), 7.

7

of the human but the natural environment as well, we may well wonder whether we have not presently come upon the moment when the old history will self-destruct.

If we need a new land, a new race, a new language, and a new mystery, it is to say, and to say fervently, that we need a new history.

I

Of course, we are not the first to sense and voice the need, although we may be among the last if the renewal of history cannot be effected. The Old Testament prophets of the eighth and seventh and sixth centuries were, in their own way, putting their bodies on the line for a new history; and our own crisis must be informed by the fact that they found the essential form and resources for the new history already present in the old. We shall come to this again. For the moment it is enough to suggest that the prophets were as obnoxious to middle Israel as today's student Left is to middle America, and that the prophets too were familiar with the devices of repression.

One ancient prophetic formulation of the new history is that still-moving statement of the new covenant in Jeremiah 31:31–34. It is not only a magnificent piece of ancient, holy utopianism, telling not what the new history will be but what it must always be in process of becoming; but also it lends itself to easy and effective appropriation from a theological to a humanistic-secular reading. The sensitive non-believer knows in his own terms what it means:

> Behold, the days are coming, says the Lord, when I will make a new covenant with the house of Israel and the house of Judah . . . : I will put my law within them, and I will write it upon their hearts; and I will be their God and they shall be my people. And no longer shall each man teach his neighbor and each his brother, saying, "Know the Lord," for they shall all know me, from the least of them to the greatest, says the Lord; for I will forgive their iniquity, and I will remember their sin no more.

The New Testament writers see the promise of the coming days of the new covenant fulfilled in Christ, and the conditions of the new history already present. Paul can say, for example, "But now we are discharged from the law, dead to that which held us captive, so that we serve not under the old written code but in the new life of the Spirit." (Rom. 7:6)

Alas, we have to say that the old history prevailed. At the same time, we know that we embrace in that dying history the promise and potential for the new life of the spirit in a new covenant, a new history, a new creation.

II

Our old history, now in the eighth decade of the twentieth century, has not only come upon a crisis of pollution, corruption, and exploitation, both human and environmental, but it is tired, it is exhausted. We shall have to ask the question, How can the old history become the new history? What are the sources and what are the forms for the renewal of history?

The profound weariness and fatigue, not to say disillusionment and disenchantment, of our very present and familiar history came to be most brilliantly portrayed in our drama and fiction, especially in the decade of the fifties, for example, in Camus and Sartre and Updike and Tennessee Williams and William Inge and James Cozzens and many others.

This passage from Camus' *The Stranger* will serve as well as anything to catch the sense of an exhausted history, exhausted of meaning, devoid of values, and in its continuation, therefore, quite absurd. The stranger, you remember, has committed an absolutely meaningless murder, is being held in prison during trial, and faces execution. In his final bitter scene with the prison chaplain, whom he has come to hate, he knows frustration and outrage because the chaplain does not understand that for the stranger *and the chaplain himself*—indeed for all men—in the midst of a history without hope and without meaning, a dark wind is forever blowing from the future.

Nothing, nothing had the least importance, and I knew quite well why. . . . From the dark horizon of my future a sort of slow, persistent breeze had been blowing toward me, all my life long, from the years that were to

come. And on its way that breeze had leveled out all
the ideas that people tried to foist on me in the equally
unreal years I then was living through. What difference
could they make to me—the deaths of others, or a
mother's love, or [this chaplain's] God; or the way a man
decides to live, the fate he thinks he chooses. . . . What
if at this very moment Marie was kissing a new boy
friend. As a condemned man himself, couldn't he grasp
what I meant by that dark wind blowing from my
future? [2]

Elsewhere the stranger recalls years on which the dark
of the future had not yet blown: "A rush of memories
went through my mind—memories of a life which was
mine no longer, and had once provided me with the
surest, humblest pleasures: warm smells of summer,
my favorite streets, the sky at evening, Marie's dresses
and her laugh." [3]

I am old enough to entertain a living memory of a
half a century. In my own lifetime I have seen us pass
from an existence of meaning, to meaninglessness, and
now to negative meaning. It is a dark wind that blows
from any future which is a projection of our old
history. It is a dark wind that not only levels the proud
structures of meaning we build and invest with a
permanence and power they do not possess but also
now threatens to destroy even the ground of the
structures.

[2] Albert Camus, *The Stranger*, tr. Stuart Gilbert (New
York: Vintage Books, 1946), 152–53.
[3] *Ibid.*, 132.

And it was the young in the sixties who said and are still saying: "We will change the projection of the future by the renewal of the present. We will disavow the heedlessness, the brutality, the dehumanization of the old history. We will give peace a chance. We will give man a chance to be man. We will open the ways for the becomingness of a new history. We will make possible the blowing of a fresh wind from the future, a sustaining wind, a freeing wind, a creative wind." And they were joined by old people and middle people, and black people and third people, and female people and poor people—and even rich people. But the weight of the old history is too much. They will be crushed and the new history lost, together with the old, if in school and church and among men of good will and men of power, we cannot increase our strength and numbers and, together, release the always latent spirit of the new covenant and the new history, for a new creation.

At the same time, there is firm and growing support of hope. The new history may already be more than latent. There is evidence that it may already be in process of becoming. The world of the university and the college appears not to be so obdurate as bitter antiestablishmentarians, younger and older, have been wont to charge. We will see in this decade the extent to which it has experienced the internal renewal of its own history.

The church, losing members and income at the

turn of the decade, may be on the point of finding its life in its willingness to lose it. As critics hold their pens at the ready eager to write the obituary of the church, that venerable institution—for all the continuing signs of bondage to the old history—may nevertheless be in process now of laying hold of a new integrity, for the new history. Pope Paul is much too slight a figure to cast an effective shadow over John. If Paul is unhappy about John's profligate squeezing of the Church's toothpaste, it is beyond the gifts of any man to put it back into the tube. One hears fresh sounds, new voices, out of conservative Protestant assemblies and publications. To accept Christ as one's personal savior is to accept as well His passion to heal the present brokenness of man. Christian faith inescapably involves responsibility for the conditions —social, economic, even political—that foster or countenance racism, poverty, or any other form of human repression. We will see, indeed we are seeing now, a growing rapprochement between "liberal" and "conservative" Protestant; and the terms themselves may be losing their heretofore firm profiles.

The old, childish theologies which for so long a time have lost the church the respect of the authentic intelligentsia of the Western world are being discarded, and even within the church we now look with gratitude on the short-lived but vigorous Death-of-God debate. As a seminary professor put it recently:

Beliefs in the God of traditional theism are now obsolete, not only because such beliefs have been fatefully compromised by the failure of the Christian institutional churches to bring forth a viable community among the peoples of mankind, but also because such beliefs correspond to a philosophical world view which is no longer compatible with the scientific discoveries of modern time. Atheism, however, means only the rejection of a certain form of theism. The so-called radical theologians of the past decade have rendered a signal service to Christian faith when they have spoken, however clumsily or notoriously, of the myth of the death of God. They meant with Friedrich Nietzsche that modern man has murdered God. This brand of atheism is genuinely compatible with the demands, the sharpness, and the scandal of biblical faith.[4]

The possibilities of the church's role in the renewal of history were excitingly in evidence at the first Assembly of the United Church of Christ held in the new decade of the 1970's. A new church president was installed, Dr. Robert Moss, formerly president of Lancaster Theological Seminary. His response was a moving, prophetic call to the whole church, and although he nowhere used the term, it was in sum an eloquent plea for a new history.

The first pioneering venture for the church should be to share fully with our youth the adventure of leading mankind into the new land. . . . The younger generation,

[4] Samuel Terrien, "Towards a New Theology of Presence," in *Union Seminary Quarterly Review,* XXIV (Spring, 1969), 229.

unbound by the ways of the culture that is passing, knows something that the older generation does not know . . . that first among the sins of the world is war.

We who are over 40 . . . can still talk about just wars and speak of wars to end war. . . . *We* remember faintly a world without military conscription. They have known nothing but military action, with only brief remissions. They entered the world as mankind developed the capacity to destroy itself. And so they see war as leading only to annihilation. . . . The biblical vision of the peaceable kingdom, the promise that men will not learn war any more will be credible to them only if the church takes an unequivocal stand that war as an instrument of national policy is unacceptable. . . .

This stand will alienate those organizations and persons who condone war as an instrument of foreign policy. So be it! The church must give its support to those who are against war and who will make the effort and take the personal risks necessary to wipe it out.

At the same assembly, Dr. Howard Spragg addressed the Board of Homeland Ministries (of which he is executive vice-president). It was a concentrated, powerful, single demand that we let nothing deter us from the mission of the church, which in this critical moment of time is effective address to the tormented condition of man. We may not be deterred by preoccupation with form and structure nor by any measure of unbelief, which has a way from time to time of plaguing us all, even the saints.

Let me give you his concluding lines.

> Salvation will come not from our pronouncements or from structure which newly reorders our lives; not alone from our good intentions or our claims to righteousness; but only by squaring our deeds with what we know to be true. It will come only through man's sensitivity to the plight of others, only through the Lord's gift of compassion, only through an understanding of the anguish which often threatens to overcome us all.
> You were hungry and I fed you. You were naked and I clothed you.
> All the rest is commentary.

When "bureaucratic" churchmen can talk like this, there is hope for a new church in a new history. There is hope for a new creation.

III

The new history is not only latent but there is evidence for hope that it is in the process of becoming. The phenomenon of our recent years that we call the generational conflict involves precisely the struggle between an old and a new history. It has a character and intensity all its own and, we may hope, ultimate consequences dramatically affecting the progress of the new history. But some of us know very well the nature of the generational conflict not only with our sons and daughters but with our own parents a generation earlier. And it is not effrontery on our part to believe that something of the new history was to be seen in us, in contrast to our fathers and mothers.

Let me briefly recall my own days of growing up and my relationship to my own parents through five decades of my life.

The second decade involved, as it always does, the long, slow, awkward, sometimes painful, process of emancipation—a process, a struggle, that in a certain sense never ends. The first decade was for me an age of total, unqualified identification with my missionary parents in China. Toward the end of my first ten years, I was sent away to the American School in Nanking, my parents being stationed down the Yangtze River and nearer Shanghai. I boarded with another missionary family and suffered such home-sickness following visits from my parents or visits with them that I sometimes thought it would be better if I never saw them at all. To be with them was to know all over again that their life was my life, their ways my way, their history my history.

We came back to the States when I was fifteen, when the process of my finding my own history was actually only just getting under way. It has been going on ever since. Through my own late twenties and through my thirties and forties we continued close, my parents and I. They became grandparents of our children and they played their part with affection; but there was mutual awareness that we were in fact living in different histories and agreement that there were matters theological and ideological that were better not discussed. When they died, in very recent years and only a couple of years apart, their book was finished and a chapter in my own was closed; and knowing the end of the book or the chapter, I can see in better perspective some of the differences in our histories. My father was an ordained minister, as I am; but we lived in different histories, and the total burden, the fundamental meaning, the essential comprehension of four monumental, staggering words tells the story of an old history and a new history. The words—God, Race, Nation, War.

My father was not a fundamentalist quite—that is, he would not have been happy in the position of defending the literal truth of every word of the Bible. On the other hand, he took a pretty dim view of anybody's chances of securing reasonable accommodations in the next life who did not see Jesus Christ as he did.

My father was a kind and compassionate man, and indignant all his life about what this country did and continued to do to the American Indian. But he was condescending to the Chinese, whom he loved and to whom he gave the most productive years of his life; and in his attitude toward Negroes (he never heard the term "Black") rather what you would expect of the son of a very wealthy Georgia landowner, and onetime slaveholder.

My father was, along with his own generation (and still today vast numbers of ours in middle America), uncritical of the arrogance of American power, of which he was both witness and beneficiary; and I think it never occurred to him to doubt the righteousness of United States intervention or aggression anywhere.

But I could not, and I cannot now, totally repudiate my father's history, for several reasons. It possessed its own qualities of enduring goodness; it embodied hopes out of which a new history could be inspired; and more than this it was, in those early years of total identification, my history. Any new history in which I stand is consciously or unconsciously, negatively or positively, in reaction or affirmation, responsible in part to the old history. If my new history is radically different at points, it is nevertheless in continuity with the old history, and it is ultimately inexplicable and meaningless if cut off from it.

IV

Four men of radical stance, passionately defining and declaring a new history, burst upon the consciousness of Palestine, and ultimately of the world, in the middle of the eighth century B.C. Any one of them was and is an explosion. Together they shook, and shake, nations and the world. They seem not to have been associated with each other—no one mentions another—but they shared the same decades in the century, the same small, long-tortured land, the same fervent persuasion that survival, to say nothing of human fulfillment, requires the renewal of man in a new history.

If we dare to listen to Amos and Hosea and Micah and Isaiah in this hour in this nation in this world, the fury of their indictment as well as its sweeping moral sensitivity exceed anything of its kind on our present scene. Thus says the Lord, the God in whom *ad nauseum* you profess to trust:

> I hate and despise the abuses of power both within and without your borders; I condemn all the wealth of a kingdom or a nation when the faces of millions continue to be ground in the dust; I heap my indignation upon you for your wanton desecration of my creation; and I vilify you for your perversion and prostitution of your fabulous endowment as son of man and son of God. Above all, I excoriate you because you give me at one and the same time iniquity *and* solemn assembly, pious profession of brotherhood, and legalized, legitimized, even systematized extortion, theft, discrimination, plunder. You give me at one and the same time protestations of peace and freedom and the perpetuation of acts of war and tyranny. My eye and my wrath are upon the sinful kingdom, and if it cannot renew its life in justice and righteousness, in mercy and humility, in compassion and integrity, it will not endure.

The fact is, obviously, that the eighth century prophets were not heeded, and the continuation of the ways of the old history led quickly to the dissolution and destruction of the old Israelite kingdom.

And the prophets wept over land and people and world. If their indictment seemed to be without mercy, it was because they cared so much for home and nation and people, because they knew their own involvement in the old history, and because they could see the new history as the fulfillment of the hopes and possibilities of the old—precisely, may I say, in the fashion of some of the young and older secular prophets of our day. The biblical prophets sometimes used the figure of the wilderness (we have its counterpart in our own formative years), the time in the life of the people, that is, before the establishment of political kingdom, of national power and prestige, of human glory. And so, God is heard to be saying, as it were: "I will take you back, and you will be what then you had hoped you might be, what was then only your promise; you will fulfill the role we had both hoped to see you play—a light to the world, an instrument for justice and peace in the world, a means of the salvation and redemption of man. Let this hope of the past be the stuff, the solid substance of a new creation and a new history."

Another prophet who came singly, starkly single, some seven hundred years later, in the same still-tortured kingdom, was saying the same thing when he said, in effect, "I did not come to destroy the old history but to fulfill it and, in fulfilling it, to put a new creation into process of becoming."

Lewis Feuer, former Berkeley social scientist now at Toronto, has written a book—a tome it is, about 550 pages, with several chapters having well over two hundred footnotes—called *The Conflict of Generations*. It is his own assessment of the character and significance of student movements around the world, up to and including Berkeley and Columbia. It is, alas, a part of the old history. Feuer's is in no sense at all a prophetic voice. In the history of student protest, he is able to see only what he calls demonry or a kind of sickness, which he describes bitterly and emotionally in these words: "The 'alienated' never looked closely into themselves to find the subjective cause of their 'alienation.' Instead, they projected upon the Impersonal Knowledge Factory and the Administration all the traits which would justify their revolt; their fruitless rebellion never reached within themselves, the inner, inaccessible Being who tyrannized over and emasculated them." [5]

There is nothing in Feuer's book to suggest the real depth and magnitude of the corruption of the old history nor any acknowledgment of the weight of provocation upon sensitive students who care with a prophetic care about home and country and world. The way to the new history does not lie in denying

[5] Lewis Feuer, *The Conflict of Generations: The Character and Significance of Student Movements* (New York: Basic Books, 1969), 467.

or ignoring all prophetic castigation because some of the prophets are wild.

V

Dr. Robert Jay Lifton of the Yale School of Medicine understands and talks about the old history and the new history. Of the present generation of young rebels, he says: "The statement they make has to do not only with social inequities and outmoded institutions, but with the general historical dislocations of everyone. And in this sense the target of the young is not so much the university, or the older generation as the continuing commitment of both to the discredited past." And further he says that "their political confrontations have achieved a number of striking successes largely because they were *not* merely assertions of will but could also mobilize a wide radius of opposition to outmoded and destructive academic and national policies."

And then, it seems to me, he comes down squarely in what I have tried to describe as the prophetic tradition. "Any New History worthy of that name," he says, "not only pits itself against, but draws actively upon, the old." Warning the young against what he calls totalism which is the denial of the principle of historical continuity, he writes:

If man is successful in creating the New History he must create if he is to have any history at all, then the formative fathers and sons must pool their resources and succeed together. Should this not happen, the failure too will be shared, whether in the form of stagnation and suffering or of shared annihilation. Like most other things in our world, the issue remains open. There is nothing absolute or inevitable about the New History, except perhaps the need to bring it into being.[6]

Speaking for myself now, but also for surprising numbers in the university and certainly for most of us in the church, I find—we find—hopes for the new history supported by the proposition of transcendence, which we are unwilling or unable to surrender. I believe: help my unbelief. It is God who makes and inspires and sends the prophets in any time. It is transcendent Being whose own divine hopes for the new creation are eloquently expressed in the whole drama of the Christ event.

If we do not know where we are going, we know what we need. We need a new history, a new creation. All too easily we recognize ourselves, man, the son of man, in the Gospel story of a healing made possible only by the response of faith. It is we, all of us, the corporate human family that is possessed of a dumb spirit, which in repeated periodic seizure casts us into the fire and into the water and threatens now as never before to destroy us. Look at our own great broken body, covered with self-inflicted wounds, man

[6] Robert Jay Lifton, "Notes on a New History. Part II, The Young and the Old," in *Atlantic Monthly*, CCXXIV (October, 1969) 83–88.

upon man—wounds of war, of racism, of arrogance, of irresponsibility, of heedlessness, of hate, and, above all, of prolonged indifference to the fact that we are one body whose health depends ultimately upon the health of all its members. If we do not know where we are going, we know what we need: we need healing and renewal for a new creation and a new history.

How long have we had this sickness, the awful sickness of man during which he has been preoccupied with the making of of injury, destruction, and death? How long have we had this sickness, we, mankind, made in the image of God and crowned with glory and honor?

Since childhood!

I hear out of what is called the generational conflict not so much the cry of arrogance and rebellion from the young, as a passionate prophetic pleading that we all believe, as they believe, that all things are possible. Healing is possible to him who believes. New creation is possible. The impossible new history is possible.

All things are possible to him who believes. In the *form* of belief which is mine, I can say it best by using the Christ image—by saying that the fully adequate resources for the new history entered time with Jesus Christ. And I would want to add that the church is doing its proper business *only* when it is celebrating the healing, creative power of his invasion of our anguished history.

But we will say, to any and all who believe, that we will work together with new hope, and with the help and promise of God, to do away with the corruption and perversion and desecration of creation and of man—so that at last it may be that all men may lie down in safety and in dignity. And God will say, "You are my people." And we will say, "He is our God."

Chapter II

BIBLICAL FOREWORD

Now the Lord said to Abram, "Go from your country and your kindred and your father's house to the land that I will show you. . . ; and by you all the families of the earth will bless themselves." (Gen. 12:1–3)

These . . . came to Egypt with Jacob . . . seventy persons; Joseph was already in Egypt. Then Joseph died, and all his brothers, and all that generation. But the descendants of Israel were fruitful and increased greatly; they multiplied and grew exceedingly strong; so that the land was filled with them.

Now there arose a new king over Egypt who did not know Joseph. . . . And the Egyptians . . . made the people of Israel serve with rigor, and made their lives bitter with hard service, in mortar and brick. . . . (Exod. 1:1–15)

[The Lord said to Moses:] "Come, I will send you to Pharaoh that you may bring forth my people, the sons of Israel, out of Egypt." (Exod. 3:10)

"When your son asks you in time to come, 'What is the meaning of the testimonies and the statutes and the ordinances which the Lord our God has commanded you?' then you shall say to your son, 'We were Pharaoh's slaves in Egypt; and the Lord brought us out of Egypt with a mighty hand . . . that he might bring us in and give us the land. . . .' " (Deut. 6:20–24)

And now [says the Lord to Isaiah], go, write it before them on a tablet, and inscribe it in a book, that it may be for the time to come as a witness forever. For they are

27

a rebellious people, lying sons, sons who will not hear the instruction of the Lord; who say to the seers, "See not"; and to the prophets, "Prophesy not to us what is right; speak to us smooth things, prophesy illusions. . . ." (Isa. 30:8–11)

The wilderness and the dry land shall be glad, the desert shall rejoice and blossom; like the crocus it shall blossom abundantly, and rejoice with joy and singing. . . . Then the eyes of the blind shall be opened, and the ears of the deaf unstopped; then shall the lame man leap like a hart, and the tongue of the dumb sing for joy. For waters shall break forth in the wilderness, and streams in the desert; the burning sand shall become a pool, and the thirsty ground springs of water; . . . No lion shall be there, nor shall any ravenous beast come up on it; they shall not be found there, but the redeemed shall walk there. (Isa. 35:1–9)

A NEW LAND: *The Campus*

IN Fowles's novel *The Magus*, young Nicholas says: "It poured with rain the day I left. But I was filled with excitement, a strange exuberant sense of taking wing. I didn't know where I was going, but I knew what I needed. I needed a new land, a new race, a new language; and, although I couldn't have put it into words then, I needed a new mystery." Well, call us all Nicholas. We do not know where

we are going, but we know what we need. We need
a new land—not necessarily a different land, but a
new land, a new campus land, a new college land, a
new university land, as well as a new American land.
We need a new race, a new race of men—not a different race, but a new race that knows itself to be one
race, one genus, one creature, one kind, one *man*. We
need a new language—not a different language, but a
new language, a language that is spoken not to be
heard but to be understood, a new language that in-
vites response and is itself responsive, a new language
whose essential word is the efficacious word, the doing
word, the word with power not to destroy but to build,
not to wound and alienate but to heal, a new language
whose effective, effecting words are responsibility and
love and redemption.

And to be sure, we need a new mystery. The old
mystery seems to have disappeared. Was it that it
proved to be too simple for us; or that we thought it
was too simple for us? Or did the keepers of the
mystery, the priests of the mystery, themselves abandon the mystery of the mystery so that their mystery
became a cliché? Or is it that all of us who are the
people of the mystery have in fact lived in denial of it,
so that the mystery has perished in the denial? Whatever its fate, the mystery appears to have lost its power,
and we need a new mystery, or at least the renewal of
the old, on which to ponder, of which to dream, and
by which to be sustained.

Paul is expressing Nicholas' sentiment, in a different way, at the end of his letter to the Galatians. And
he says it with fire and force and passion—and brevity.
He has been dictating the letter, but now he takes
the pen himself and writes, as it were, in italics. For
Paul there is an irrepressible urgency now about the
new land and the new race and the new language
and the new mystery in Christ; he wants the new
Christians in Galatia to be coming along, and they're
hung up on the tired, obsolete, irrelevant forms of
the old world symbolized in the debate on circumcision. Paul explodes: "Circumcision is nothing. Uncircumcision is nothing. The only thing that counts
is new creation!" (Gal. 6:15, NEB)

And like Paul, and long before him, a prophet
standing at the end of that sustained, two-century
explosion into the world of the classical Old Testament prophets is taken with a vision of new creation
—"New things I now declare; before they spring
forth, I tell you of them!" (Isa. 42:9) And speaking
as if he were himself the timeless Doer, the one
eternal Actor, he cries, "I am doing a new thing;
now it springs forth, do you not perceive it? I will
make a way in the wilderness and rivers in the desert."
(Isa. 43:19)

New creation. A way in the wilderness. Rivers in the
desert. Order and direction out of chaos. The water
of life over the parched sands of death. Responsibility

in place of responselessness; identity out of anonymity; full personhood in place of dehumanization; compassion where there was heedlessness; imagination, sensitivity, and identification instead of the facelessness of pride; and peace and healing out of estrangement.

Ways in the wilderness. Rivers in the desert. A new creation!

I

We do not know where we are going, but we know what we need.

Now, the man wise in the ways of this world, the man of prudence, the realist, would say that Nicholas and Paul and the prophets are all mad. Nicholas, he might say, would more wisely settle for a try at a new land, maybe, or a new mystery—never mind a race and a language. Paul, he would argue, is out of his mind to say that nothing, absolutely nothing, matters except new creation; and it is simply prophetic fever that talks about the conquest of the impenetrable, uncharted wilderness and the redemption of the desert of the environment and psyche of man.

Nicholas, of course, is young, and we oldsters can say, and we're saying it *ad nauseum*, that Nicholas had better make his peace with things as they are, with the world as it is. Paul and the prophets are a very different matter and we can excuse them. Paul had Christ, or Christ had Paul, and that takes care of that. And the prophet? It was easy for him. He shared the vivid memory of the creation of his people out of the nonbeing of Egypt, and long before that he knew of the creation of order out of cosmic chaos —together, two attested facts of new creation. Why not now, and easily, a third?

In the biblical perspective it can always be, even if it is humanly impossible; and even in a predominantly secular point of stand, it can be and it must be, even if it cannot wholly be. Whether we take one or the other position, we can agree that it is imperative that we find together a new land, a new race, a new language, and a new mystery. And we will agree tentatively that the way to new creation is in the creative word. We will agree that new creation is all that matters now, and that the efficacious Word with a capital W exists by which we may find our way out of the wilderness and make our deserts, wherever they are, blossom like the rose.

II

The only thing that counts is new creation. We need a new land. The American campus must become—is becoming, willy-nilly—a new land. The Word, whatever its source, is as clear as it was to Abraham. "Leave your country, your family and your father's house, for the land I will show you" (Gen. 12:1, JB). Or, because American higher education is to some extent undeniably enslaved by the old ways of country, family, and father's house, and by the devices of what may legitimately be called Pharaoh-ism, the Word is essentially and urgently the Word to Moses, "Bring my people out of Egypt!"

The fact is that a new king has arisen, a new climate has set in, a new world has been imposed, which knows not Joseph—or Abe or Mary or Peter or Sue. And on the campus as in Egypt, we know that we cannot live with namelessness.

I remember a preschool mistake in memorization that occurred some years ago in the case of a faculty child at Yale, who, having heard the Lord's Prayer repeatedly, was herself heard to say it as she believed she had heard it: "Our Father, who art in New Haven, how did you know my name?"

Namelessness and its twin facelessness are not simply a matter of size, although figures on the growth of the educational establishment are staggering. In 1939, 14 percent of the eighteen-to-twenty-two-year-old group was in college. Today it is pushing very close to 50 percent. Or, to put it in numbers, students totaled about one and a third million in 1940. We have now passed seven million. Of course, size makes more difficult the preservation of the person as person. One competent educational analyst believes that the Berkeley explosions beginning in 1964 "can in large part be attributed to exploited undergraduates who were valued not as students to be educated, but as statistical numbers to generate increasing budget support." [1]

The fact is that devices do exist within the large university—for example, the system of residential colleges, schools, small units—to cope with the problem of sheer numbers. Real recognition of face and name, meaningful response of person to person, all too often fails even when name and face are known. To an alarming degree we are a society, not of persons, but of type, color, profession and function. A kind of contempt of person as person—or perhaps even a *fear* of personness—has invaded our classrooms and common rooms and offices, and even our bedrooms where we responsibly confront neither ourselves nor whomever shares our space.

It is serious enough when the person is lost as person in the bureaucracy of government or business. When practical namelessness takes the campus, when Pharaoh no longer knows Joseph, and Joe no longer knows Barbara or Tim, it is time to move, it is time to get out of Egypt and take a new land.

The depersonalization of the campus occurs not only by infection from an increasingly dehumanized social environment but by the traditional rigidity of

[1] From a preprinted version of "Aggiornamento in Higher Education," delivered by H. D. Gideonse, at the annual conference of the Association of College Unions-International, Benjamin Franklin Hotel, Philadelphia, Pennsylvania, April 12, 1967.

the campus institution. We are captive, as Abraham was, of the ways of the house of our fathers; or, to change the figure, we are victims of the preoccupation with making brick. The fathers of the university, or the Pharaohs of this land we are in, like the presiding elders of any establishment, are, naturally, advocates of the schemes and ways by which they came to be where they are. Criteria of faculty evaluation and of promotion and tenure by which they ascended the academic ladder have at least the authority of the stone tablets of Sinai and, in any case, in the making of brick they have proved themselves to be unexcelled.

The fact is that the rigidity, emphases, and indoctrination of graduate schools in which faculty are trained—or should we say certified?—as well as the prevailing schemes of faculty evaluation and promotion effectively *restrain* the teacher from engaging himself as a full human being in the life of the campus community. We are moving on this but, as in so many areas of our corporate life, in perilously slow motion. A few years ago, in response to vigorous student protest against the University's failure to give tenure to a brilliant teacher of philosophy and a highly supportive campus citizen, Yale appointed an ad hoc committee on policies and procedures in matters of tenure appointments. The subsequent report, named for its chairman the Dahl Report, was and has been widely applauded because in subtle ways it recognized and sought to alleviate the campus problem of depersonalization. As in this sentence: "Unusually effective teaching or an unusually large contribution to the community's well-being will serve as strong supports for the evidence of quality provided by the candidate's scholarly writing." Cheers for this! And no one will take exception when the report adds: "But this cannot compensate for a total absence of the most tangible and enduring demonstration of a scholar's distinction." But increasing numbers of us, students and faculty, would recommend the turning about of these statements from the Dahl Report: "The most distinguished demonstration of scholarly distinction cannot compensate for a total absence of concern for effective teaching and the whole life of the student who is taught; nor can it compensate for the virtual abdication of any significant role which contributes to the community's well-being."

A former president of Stanford was a noted ichthyologist, reputed to know the scientific names of more fish than anyone else in the world. Asked once if he did as well with students, he replied, "Oh, my, no. I don't even try. Every time I remember the name of a student I forget the name of a fish."

In the new land of learning to which we on the campus are urgently called, Joseph will be remembered, the conditions of namelessness alleviated, and the devices that diminish the qualities of the full person, that hamper the realization of full community will be corrected. Brick will continue to be produced, but the *whole* brick-producing company will understand why we are making brick. And brick making will serve the ultimate ends of making man.

A Harvard report asks the question, How do we restore to the center of our academic programs the interest in educating men and women who will be fit for the moral and intellectual responsibilities of a free society; and the report responds: "The key might lie in a better understanding of human values. It is the individual human being, ultimately, that is the carrier of value." Charles Malik said the same thing more fervently when he wrote: "We need a passion for the intimate, for gentleness, for love. These are gifts of the spirit, attitudes of the soul . . . these gifts pass from person to person, and when there is no *person* who has them, then they simply cannot be had." [2]

III

Exodus was and is from namelessness, from facelessness, from the loss of personness and the sense of the value of the person.

Exodus and the call to a new land is also always away from powerlessness. "We were Pharaoh's *slaves* in Egypt" runs the cultic refrain. To a certain degree it is true that all of us who make up the campus scene —trustees and administration as well as students and faculty—are victims of an enslaving institutional

---

[2] Charles Malik, "Reflections on the Great Society," in *Saturday Review*, August 6, 1966, pp. 12–15.

Pharaohism which deprives us all of essential power. But that is another story for another day. The most conspicuous feature of our time, this hectic moment of history, is the coincident plurality and ferocity of the revolt of the powerless. Powerlessness with self-consciousness leads to impotence, impotence to rage, and rage to violence—among women, among blacks, among the poor, and among students on the campus.

As in the first Exodus, a greater problem, I think, than even the most radical leadership is the problem of the apathetic. The corporate memory of the Israelite bid for a new land recalls multitudes of the company (one takes it, most of the company) crying, almost before they have begun, for the old, comfortable status of dependence and the steady perquisites thereof. As the ancient saga has it, "every family at the door of its tent" was wailing, "Who will give us meat to eat? . . . Think of the fish we used to eat free in Egypt, the cucumbers, melons, leeks, onions and garlic! Here we are wasting away, stripped of everything; . . ." (Num. 11:4–6, JB) So too, on the American campus. While their numbers are surely diminishing, there are still the apathetic who are content to make brick without straw, to stay away from the whip, and to receive the rewards of the system, the onions and garlic of the proper grades, the proper courses, the proper degrees, and the proper jobs.

But the Exodus occurred and it will occur even without their support, or in spite of them. The old state of powerlessness has become intolerable for a number of human groups, students among them, that have overnight come of age. The obvious question until now has been whether the possibilities of a new land may not be destroyed in the madness and violence to become freed of the old.

Suppose we ask now, What is the student powerless to do that he wants to do? or Why does he now want power on the campus when those who went before him, say, in the 1950's, were relatively content with the ways of Pharaohism? It may be worth remembering that student attempts to seize or exercise power are in fact as old as the very institution. Activist student violence was common in the medieval university; and to take an unlikely American illustration, staid, proper old Princeton had no fewer than six major student rebellions in the early 1800's, in one of which students set fire to the very building in which at the moment the faculty was meeting! Imagine! Princeton long ago out-Berkeleyed Berkeley!

Why now so strong a bid for student power? The fact is that from 1964 to the end of the decade of the sixties, American campuses suffered disruption in unprecedented number and, at least in this century, with unequaled violence. What happened? The reigning and, some of us felt, ominous quiet characteristic of the campus in the fifties was brought to an end in the civil rights movement of the sixties. The suddenly aroused and mortified conscience of students led them in large numbers to support and participate in programs of action in the South, some of them technically illegal and aimed at breaking hard-set patterns of segregation. I think the results will appear in the long run to have been far more effective than they knew. A young black woman has written in a prize-winning essay:

> What good was the civil rights movement? If it had just given this country Dr. King, a leader of conscience for once in our lifetime, it would have been enough. . . . If it gave us nothing else, it gave us each other forever. It gave some of us bread, some of us shelter, some of us knowledge and pride, all of us comfort. It gave us our children, our husbands, our brothers, our fathers, as men reborn and with a purpose for living. It broke the pattern of black servitude in this country. It shattered the phony "promise" of white soap operas that sucked away so many pitiful lives. It gave us history and men far greater than Presidents. It gave us heroes, selfless men of courage and strength, for our little boys to follow. It gave us hope for tomorrow. It called us to live.[3]

Nevertheless, campus activism in the civil rights arena slowed to a discouraged halt until its energies were redirected in even more voluble and violent protest against the Vietnam war and, especially since the death of Dr. King, against white racism.

It should have been plain to us all along that we

[3] Alice Walker, "The Civil Rights Movement: What Good Was It?" in *American Scholar*, XXXVII (Autumn, 1968), 27.

were witnessing the birth of a new student morality; and one can and must say unequivocally that the contemporary student rejection of powerlessness is in part, and significantly, morally motivated. It was sorely aggrieved morality that sparked, at least, insurrectionist scenes at Columbia and Stanford and Berkeley and on a dozen other campuses. Indeed, no major student uprising I know of was without a strong motivation in moral outrage. We are seeing as never before a new, sensitive, comprehensive humanism that may even be called religious but not, of course, in any formal sense of the word, nor, particularly, in any institutional or theological sense. Not many university students see themselves as in any meaningful way "belonging" to the Church or the Synagogue or the Temple. Their temper of mind is prevailingly agnostic, an open, gentle agnosticism, an agnosticism I find on the whole highly compassionate and tentative—and this is as it should be.[4] The notions of God that reached them earlier, they would say, are for the birds (as well, indeed, some of them probably were!). But if the Three Letters can be stretched entirely out of the old shapes, God very much is—in justice and compassion and love; in the struggle of black and white, ghetto with suburb, integrity with hypocrisy, peace with war, life with death. Certainly, students

---

[4] One observes a phenomenal surge of interest among students in Eastern religions. See, e.g., Jacob Needleman, *The New Religions* (New York: Doubleday and Co., 1970).

in larger proportion than ever before embrace now
an authentic, courageous morality that sees immorality—some of them would call it obscenity—where it
really is: in any and all forms of dehumanization, in
any and all schemes and devices that thwart the realization of full humanity anywhere. They do not quite
know what to do with the first great commandment—
Thou shalt love the Lord thy God with all thy heart—
but increasing numbers of them are broadly and passionately committed to the second—Thou shalt love
thy neighbor as thyself.

These contemporary campus generations are possessed of a still-growing sense of indignation at the
immorality of the inherited world, and that indignation was turned on the university itself, in unprecedented demands for a voice and for power to influence
decisive and, if need be, radical change.

In a review of Jencks and Riesman's *Academic
Revolution*, Martin Duberman, the author of *In
White America*, helps explain this. Student radicals,
he points out, are far more disenchanted with the
educational establishment than Jencks and Riesman.

> Their disgust with traditional procedures is grounded
> in a growing distrust of rationality itself, of the im-
> portance of gathering and transmitting factual informa-
> tion and technical expertise. They are angry because
> they know that their growth depends on more than the
> accumulation of information. The kind of growth they
> value—increased openness to a range of experience,

emotional honesty, personal interaction—seems actually threatened and compromised by additional proficiency in the manipulation of ideas and things. . . . Or as Berger, one of the hippie heroes of "Hair" succinctly puts it to his teachers: "Screw your logic and reason." The rationalist tradition, as the student rebels see it, has produced a race of deformed human beings, or rather, a race of thinking machines: heads (the old-fashioned kind) without bodies or feelings. The new generation does not wish men to become mindless; they wish them to become something more than minds.[5]

One of the bitterest chapters in the history of American higher education was written in the spring of 1968 at Columbia University. It may still be too soon to assess the full meaning of that devastating upheaval. We are only now beginning to read with understanding the story of Berkeley's human storm which began some years ago. The first chapter in the same book now embraces Columbia and Stanford and Harvard and M.I.T. and scores of other campuses across the country, and most recently and most tragically also includes Kent State and Jackson State. But one thing is clear, whatever ultimate judgments are made: it is monumentally naïve and simplistic to read all this as simply the arbitrary explosion of arrogant, undisciplined, malevolent, and destructive young people, to be met in the future with always

[5] Martin Duberman, "Exploring the Academy," in *New Republic*, June 22, 1968, pp. 27–28.

harder, more stringent, more immediate, and more vindictive retribution.

The way from Berkeley to Stanford to Columbia to Harvard to the present defines not only growing student outrage over the immorality of environmental pollution, of racism, and of war but over what some of our brightest and most responsible students have come to see as the sometimes prostitution of the university itself, its selling itself, and inevitably its students and faculty, to the uses of its customers, its clients, its exploitative and powerful clientele; or, in the language of the Exodus allegory, its unprotesting conformity to alien demands, its acquiescence in Pharaohism.

The revolt against powerlessness, the press for student power, is to be sure for some few students a bid for power for its own sake; but for more, far more—and it is these who count—it is a desperate plea to be given an effective role in shaping now and for the future the function and psyche and purposes of the new university.

IV

And the students *are* being heard. In President Kingman Brewster's annual report published in 1968, he recalls the event to which earlier I referred, the failure of the University to retain a highly effective teacher. As a faculty witness to, and even sympathetic participant in, the student protest at that time, I would not have believed that it could for the short or long run, effectively influence university policy. But here is Brewster:

> In retrospect I now count Yale extremely fortunate to have been awakened to the vital concern of the current generation of students for the quality of their Yale education by the well publicized case of a popular philosophy teacher who was not promoted to tenure in 1965. Not just exhibitionists, agitators, and *News* pundits, but scores of academic and extracurricular achievers and swarms of average undergraduates poured out their concern for the standards and procedures for faculty appointment and promotion. The disposition of the particular case was not the most important aspect. Even the very salutary "Dahl Report" which reappraised appointment standards and procedures was not the most significant outcome. The most crucial impact was the message to the entire Yale community, especially to the faculty, that we were henceforth in a new era in which students demanded and deserved respect for their views about how to improve Yale education.

This administrative sentiment prevails, or is coming to prevail, in colleges and universities all across the country.

If one speaks with compassion, as I have tried to do, of the contemporary student's protests against powerlessness from Berkeley to Columbia to where we are right now, one does not justify all forms of expression of protest or all protesters. In every disruptive campus rebellion, the student demagogue emerges, as also the one who is exploiting the event to ease or adjust or modify an ill-fitting identity, or even the real revolutionary who *genuinely* wants the establishment brought down in ruins. The bitterness and anger of a few, their arrogance, their apparent repudiation of compassion, and their sometimes appalling posture of self-righteousness—all this one sees and deplores. Most profoundly, one regrets that sometimes the protesting student acts as if the university acquired all its unworthy characteristics through the sheer perversity and deliberate malice of an evil coalition of administrators and trustees, when, in reality, these persons have for the most part responded to total university demands in the best light given them.

The fact is that the now-parallel acts of rebellion against the nameless, the faceless, the voiceless, the powerless human condition are a part of the inevitable eruptions from our deep human sickness, our virtually total human brokenness. All of us in the university, and even more in this country, have been saying too long what in ancient Israel the people said to their prophets: "Do not prophesy to us right things—speak to us smooth things, prophesy illusions!" The fever that burns on the campus, in the nation, and in the world will not subside tomorrow. We will never be the same again. The present trial of the university betrays the excruciating frustration of the young who, with reason, do not believe that they are *really* known, seen, recognized, and heard; and who believe that moral abuse is heaped on moral abuse by the nation's refusal to hear and understand their cry as a moral protest against perversion and inhumanity and servitude.

Student refusal to continue in a powerless state mirrors, finally, the continuing scandal of white preoccupation with a relatively dwindling white world. It holds up in vivid relief the unspeakable genocide of our times. And it cries out, especially in its recent course, against all forms of the prostitution of learning and the debasing of the community of learners.

President Hitch of the University of California spoke these words before the California Board of Regents: "We have to be steady enough to face the fact that the trouble of our time is rooted in past inequalities and injuries, and we have to be wise enough to work for the elimination of the angry frustrations of many, the indifference of many more, and the fears that are corroding the institution. . . . This [current] trouble will be with us until every man is allowed his full measure of human dignity. We must be as large in spirit as these times demand."

We began in search of a Word, the Word. We will continue in that search. I have given you words, many words, possibly only words. Or perhaps it may be that in all of these words, there is embedded the attested, valid human word and even a whisper of the ultimately authentic Word.

Chapter III

BIBLICAL FOREWORD

Now Moses was keeping the flock of his father-in-law, Jethro, the priest of Midian; and he led his flock to the west side of the wilderness, and came to Horeb, the mountain of God. And the angel of the Lord appeared to him in a flame of fire out of the midst of a bush; and he looked, and lo, the bush was burning, yet it was not consumed. And Moses said, "I will turn aside and see this great sight, why the bush is not burnt." When the Lord saw that he turned aside to see, God called to him out of the bush, "Moses, Moses!" And he said, "Do not come near; put off your shoes from your feet, for the place on which you are standing is holy ground. . . . I have seen the affliction of my people who are in Egypt . . . and I have come . . . to bring them up out of that land to a good and broad land, a land flowing with milk and honey, . . . Come, I will send you to Pharaoh that you may bring forth my people . . . out of Egypt. (Exod. 3:1–10)

A NEW RACE: *The Nation*

W E do not know where we are going, but we know what we need. We need a new land, a new race, a new language; and although we will have trouble putting it into words, we need a new mystery.

We need a new land, a new educational environment; not a different land but a renewed land, a renewed campus, where name and face are really known and where the frustrations and outrage of powerlessness are removed in a community of learning shaped by the responsible, responsive, compassionate participation of a maximum number of its members and all of its component groups. In the new school land —in the Exodus analogy—bricks, the stuff of constructive work, will be produced but in forms and shapes and methods to which all consent, and to the end not simply of producing brick but of producing man in full human stature.

We need a new race; not a different race, but a renewed race, in St. Paul's phrase, a people "not conformed to this world, but . . . transformed by the renewal of their mind." Or, as Paul would say it directly to us: "Adapt yourselves no longer to the pattern of this present world, but let your minds be remade and your whole nature thus transformed. Then you will be able to discern the will of God, and to know what is good, acceptable, and perfect." (Rom. 12:2, NEB) This is the same man who says, you remember, "Circumcision is nothing. Uncircumcision is nothing. The only thing that counts is new creation!"

The prophet, it is Ezekiel in this case, looks at a conforming people, an essentially sterile national environment, a land whose inhabitants have lost the power of perception and whose notions of what is good and acceptable and perfect reflect only the perversion, banality, and cruelty of a grossly inequitable culture. Ezekiel looks at his own immediate race, his own people, and he sees nothing for it but a massive corporate heart transplant operation, with God as the declarer and chief surgeon: "I will give them one heart, and put a new spirit within them; I will take the stony heart out . . . and give them a heart of flesh . . . and they shall be my people and I will be their God." (Ezek. 11:19–20)

Later, the prophet's own cry is angry and urgent: "Get yourselves a new heart and a new spirit! Why will you die, O house of Israel?" Still later the prophetic compassion turns again, perhaps in despair of human effort, to the word and act of God: "I shall pour clean water over you and you will be cleansed; I shall cleanse you of all your defilement and all your idols. I shall give you a new heart, and put a new spirit in you; I shall remove the heart of stone from your bodies and give you a heart of flesh instead. I will be your God." (36:25–28, JB)

There is something of Nicholas and Paul and the prophet in all of us, even those in whom the symptoms of a stony heart are most conspicuous. Robert Frost's perennial man who says, "Good fences make good neighbors"; the readers of Ayn Rand; Wallace supporters; Klansmen; Birchers; followers of "Christian" (please, that word in quotes: what a monstrously fraudulent use of the term) purveyors of hate like B. J. Hargis, C. W. Burpo, and Carl McIntire—even some of these may not be unreachable, impervious, to talk of a new heart and a new spirit.

And if there is any truth at all in this, then there is ground for hope, because on the campus now there are students in large and growing numbers who will play Pharaoh's games no longer; and in between them and the virulent Right, or for that matter the nihilist Left, there are millions of this American race of ours— large numbers of them in the churches—who are ready to respond to efforts at renewal, transformation, new creation, and new heart and spirit.

I

The campus' role of leadership and that of the church are, of course, absolutely crucial. Not a few contemporary prophets will tell us that if the university and the church cannot redeem themselves from their own bondage to the ways of the fathers, the production of lifeless brick, and to conformity to the regimen of the domineering culture then we will, so to speak, never get out of Egypt. We are lost as a people.

I cannot go as far as some secularists do, who simply throw the whole messianic mantle over the shoulders of the university. I serve two institutions, the university and the church; and while I have my moments of vast discouragement about both, I see in the one the irrepressible power of man to be whole man and in the other what I can regard only as the clear survival of God. Or, to turn it about, I am above all supported in these most terrible and magnificent years by what I can see only as the participating life of God in the secular campus and the new passion for the life of humanity in the Holy Church Universal.

Walter Lippmann has invested the university with the role of new messiah. In a single article he speaks a number of times of the sure demise of the old order, and of the sole, exclusive, unique power of the university to save mankind and the world. Here, for example, he writes: "One of the great phenomena of the human condition in the modern age is the dissolution of the ancestral order, the erosion of established authority; and, having lost the light and leading, the guidance and support, the discipline that the ancestral order provided, modern men are haunted by a feeling of being lost and adrift, without purpose and meaning in the conduct of their lives. The thesis which I am putting to you is that the modern void must be filled, and that the universities must fill the void because they alone can fill it." This sounds almost like the language of nineteenth century Protestant evangelism! Elsewhere in the same article, Lippmann underlines his conviction that only the university can save, saying: "as men become modern men, they are emancipated and thus deprived of the guidance and support of traditional and customary authority. Because of this, there has fallen to the universities a unique, indispensable and capital function in the intellectual and spiritual life of modern society." [1]

In effect, Lippmann wants the university to play the role of Moses the Deliverer to the whole family of contemporary man. Let us look, then, at the old Exodus saga again. If we can put aside questions of the historical credibility, the "facticity" of the narrative and let it serve us without inhibition at least as a moving and instructive parable, we must observe first of all that Moses, while deprived in Midianite exile of the plush life of Egyptian royalty, is hardly suffering the pangs of privation here with Jethro. He is, to be sure, even more effectively removed than before from his own people, that race "lost and adrift, without purpose and meaning in the conduct of their lives . . . deprived of the guidance and support of traditional and customary authority." But then this becomes the ivory tower par excellence! The Egyptian draft cannot reach him here. He is a favored son-in-law living in the pleasant tents of a powerful chieftain and priest, with guarantees of tenure from church and state, as it were. He has an assured future with the promise, if he stays and plays the chieftain-priest's game, of ever-larger flocks and herds.

[1] Walter Lippmann, "The University," in New Republic, May 28, 1966, pp. 17–20.

Except—then and now—he and we are confronted by the burning bush, the bush that burns and is not consumed, the fiery bush out of which voices come, and words; or a Voice, and a Word. Vietnam is still burning. Poverty is burning. The black man's bitterness is burning—and the white man's hate. Conformity and apathy continue to burn and are not consumed; and smugness and hypocrisy persist. The emptiness of our national jargon continues to be inflamed. We see in the bush our derailment as a people, our bondage as men to purposes that are humanly debilitating, degrading, demeaning. And the voices, or the Voice, the words, or the Word, are of Holy Ground, set apart for the uses of God and man, prepared for the redemption of a nation, a people, a race. And the Word on this Holy Ground, to Moses, and to the university and the church, the Word out of the burning bush is that our Horeb, our campus, our church, our Midianite sojourn is quite simply accursed if the tower is sustained, if a kind of life tenure is claimed, if the lost are abandoned and Egypt ignored.

II

Life with academic Jethro—and the enormity of its indifference to human bondage when no burning bush is confronted—struck me one recent summer day when my wife and I were talking with a Stanford graduate student. Depending upon where you yourself stand, you might call him a radical, a member of the New Left. But then I don't know what this means. He is not a Communist. He is not a nihilist. He is not a destroyer. But he takes, I think with some justification, a pretty dim view of what by and large we are; and he possesses a consuming vision of what, on the campus and in this nation and world, we might be. We were talking, the three of us, of environment and race and war and politics; of human passion; of love and hate and our total, vast, awesome, frightening, infuriating predicament—when in walked two young friends of ours, fresh graduates of a prestigious eastern university, taking a leisurely domestic sight-seeing junket before entering the medical school of a prestigious eastern university in the fall. Now I want to tell you what happened. The burning bush went out. The conversational climate changed at once to the insipid. These were Jethro's boys, nice guys; I think you have to say good guys, informed to be sure—but not engaged and not about to be really engaged even sympathetically in bloody turmoil; nice guys, I say, but given our Egypt and their fundamental indifference to it, crippled or maimed or stunted. I think the damage is irreversible. The tragedy for them and for us and for the race is unspeakable, immeasurable.

We need a new race, a race not conformed to the pattern of this present world, but with minds remade and very nature transformed. The only thing that counts is new creation, a new heart, a new spirit.

To teachers of the Old Testament or for that matter, I suppose, to students who have been subjected
to an academic run through its pages, it is a tired
epigram that Moses' task was not simply to get Israel
out of Egypt, but to get Egypt out of Israel. The contemporary black leader knows precisely what this is.
It is one task to get the blacks out of the ghetto. It is
another immediate and simultaneous pursuit to get
the ghetto out of the black, to replace mental bondage
to Negroness with pride in black and dignity in full
human stature. The old status, the old ways of father's
house, the habituated cultural patterns yield reluc-
tantly to the always excruciatingly painful process of
transformation, new creation—the ultimate acquisi-
tion of new heart and new spirit.

If we propose to be in fact engaged in the life of the
race and if we really believe that the only thing that
counts is new creation, then it will be well if we know
what we are up against. We must assess realistically
the task, at least as seemingly impossible as that of
Moses, of getting the race out of Egypt and Egypt
out of the race, the people out of bondage, and the
heart and spirit of bondage out of the people.

The peculiar conditions of our own American
bondage may be assessed in three more or less catastrophic failures. I have no doubt that these had their
counterparts, for very different reasons, among the
people of Jacob and Joseph, and among any people
who have in some sense lost their freedom and whose

powers to achieve new creation have been suppressed
or depleted or destroyed.

III

The first is the failure of sympathy. I mean sympathy in none of its sentimental or purely emotional
uses, but specifically in the definition (*Webster's Third
New International Dictionary*) "the act or capacity
of entering into or sharing the feelings or interests
of another." In biblical terms it is the failure to fulfill
the second great commandment: it is the loss of the
act and capacity of love of neighbor. In Ezekiel's
terms, we are talking about the stony heart.

It is clearly what Benjamin DeMott of Amherst
College is talking about under the title "America the
Unimagining." [2] We—our culture, our people—are
fearfully indicted in DeMott's quotation of Sartre,
who says, "there are men who die without—save for
brief and terrifying flashes of illumination—ever having suspected what the *Other* is"; and of Max
Scheler, who says: "Love calls explicitly for an understanding entry into the individuality of *another* person *distinct in character* from the entering self . . . a
warm and whole-hearted endorsement of 'his' reality
as an individual, and 'his' being what he is." If this is
love, it is clear that ours is a colossal failure.

DeMott suspects what I have myself long suspected,

[2] Benjamin DeMott, "America the Unimagining," in
American Scholar, XXXVII (Summer, 1968), 409–19.

that in this respect Emerson has done us no good at all. Men of my profession (I mean now Protestant preachers) have found him eminently quotable but, as it has seemed to me, invariably in antithesis to biblical-prophetic passion. "In Emerson," DeMott says, "self-fulfillment appears to require an absolute denial of others, a massive, unrelenting independence, a readiness for isolation." And he offers this superb piece of Emersonia: "At times the whole world seems to be in conspiracy to importune you with emphatic trifles. [God, what *trifles* these are!] Friend, client, child, sickness, fear, want, charity, all knock at once at the closet door, and say, 'Come out unto us.' But keep thy state; come not into their confusion."

For whatever reasons, and they are many—(De-Mott also speaks of the preoccupation of our general culture with "feats of objectification"), we suffer a general failure of sympathy, of sympathetic imagination. The condition may be fatal. It has already brought us hate and violence. It is indirectly responsible for the murder and assassination of Medgar Evers, John F. Kennedy, Malcolm X, James Reeb, Viola Liuzzo, Martin Luther King, Jr., and Robert F. Kennedy, to name only a few. It may yet undo us. Meanwhile, the unrelieved personal tragedy of the failure of sympathy is this: except as I enter the feelings and interests of the other—every other who confronts me —I remain myself stunted, truncated, unfulfilled. If the campus and the church cannot shake this bondage, if Moses cannot lead, there is no possibility of a new people, a new creation.

IV

A second pervasive expression of our bondage is the failure of perception. We have surrendered to a widely homogenized, single-flavored, single-textured culture the power to make, assert, and act upon vigorous and even passionate personal, private, and individual distinctions. As a people, one suspects, we have largely lost the capacity to pursue what Socrates regarded as the ultimate end of man—to choose one's own destiny, and to gain "the ability and intelligence to know a good life from a bad."

Erich Fromm, having referred to all the talk of the death of God, goes on to say: "But what we confront now is the possibility that man is dead, transformed into a thing, a producer, a consumer, an idolator of other things. . . . A man sits in front of a bad television program and does not know that he is bored; he reads of Viet Cong casualties in the newspaper and does not recall the teachings of religion; he learns of the dangers of nuclear holocaust and does not feel fear; he joins the rat race of commerce, where personal worth is measured in terms of market values, and is not aware of his anxiety." [3]

To an extent quite beyond the awareness of most of

[3] Erich Fromm in "News and Notes," in *Pastoral Psychology*, XVII (April, 1966).

us, we submit—if perception is to be exercised, if distinctions are to be made—to the pervasive monochrome, accustomed, middle-American culture mass. Let me put it bluntly. This failure to assert the rights and consequences of private perception, this acquiescence in a kind of national moral decision making, will inexorably undo us, if we are not already undone. With our own rights of perception surrendered or, who knows, quietly annulled, we appear as a people to have been lulled into believing that it's all right, Joe; that you can somehow remain a human being while you live and move and exist in a dehumanized environment; that you can retain your status as a person in a society that is appallingly depersonalized; in short, that the distorted, reduced, shattered, warring, hating, corrupting, polluting, bleeding image of man is *natural*.

If we on the campus or in the church are to be in some meaningful sense Moses to a people in bondage and if as a people we are to get us a new heart and be a new creation, then one thing is clear. Neither the university nor the church can conform to the tyrannical controls of a cultural Pharaohism. Its members will have to be nourished in such a way that the trance of enslavement is broken and the power of perception that is distinction, evaluation, judgment, and consequent action is exercised again in freedom.

Chancellor Gideonse, of the New School for Social Research, demanding a better understanding of human values in education, declares that this will call "first of all for an education that will be the opposite of education 'consistent with the culture' that is now so fashionable in respectable academic circles. It will call for an education that will seek to correct or to offset many of the cultural influences that are increasingly exercised by the society itself." [4]

We require, do we not, what Berthold Brecht called the estrangement effect, by which he means any device of perception which gives us power to break through the massively sponsored stereotypes and illusions about things and people and the world? Brecht tells us that this estrangement effect is a function of art. And so it is. But it must also be a function of education and religion. The estrangement effect is again to produce a dissociation in which what is observed is recognized for what it is, not what it is said to be. As Brecht puts it, in the estrangement effect "the things of everyday life are lifted out of the realm of the self-evident (and) that which is 'natural' assumes the features of the extraordinary." [5]

The failure of sympathy and the failure of perception is the failure of humanity, the failure of humanness. I am with the students of this generation who are trying to bring the university—and the church, if it will listen—out of bondage. I am with the students

[4] Gideonse, "Aggiornamento in Higher Education."
[5] As quoted in Herbert Marcuse, *One-Dimensional Man* (Boston: Beacon Press, 1964), 67.

who are crying to us all now that it's not all right, Joe. It's all wrong when evil is spelled with a capital C for Communism, when black man and black woman are unmanned and unwomanned, when death is spread like poison on the bread of life, when life is death by the design of the living, when hate is not spontaneous but cultivated, when law and order take priority over justice and love. I am with the students who are saying, "It'll be all right, Joe, only when peace is peace, and compassion compassion, and persons are persons, and life is life."

V

Briefly now, along with decrying the failure of sympathy and perception, we make note of what appears to be the increasing failure of corporate celebration. Robert Theobald puts his own suspicion of this failure in hypothetical form. How ought people, he asks, to mark the change "from one state in their life pattern . . . to another, from being a young person to an adult, from being unmarried to married? Our society does not dramatize change in life style. Weddings, for example, have become just a vestige of what they were and many persons are very impatient even with the vestige. We must examine once more whether we need to dramatize changes in the situation of a person." But Theobald goes further. We must reconsider, he says, "the implications of our complete destruction of all celebrations. We have a lot of holidays, but they are not community celebrations in any sense." And then he asks, "Does a living and vibrant community require some occasions on which it meets together and celebrates the fact that it exists as a community?" [6]

Theobald professes not to know the answer and neither do I. We would both emphatically exclude from the category of celebration, as we mean it, much in American life that passes for celebration—sports events, the likes of Elks conventions, or such immense, manipulated, chauvinistic gatherings as occurred in Washington on July 4, 1970. But it is clear that no community long survives without the support of the cultic/ritual act, the celebration not simply of the fact of community, but the meaning, the shared memory, the mutual affection and responsibility, the uniqueness and call of *this* community, large or small, the celebration of what and who and why *we* are. Without it, the psyche of a people withers; indeed, as numbers of psychiatrists will testify, the individual who loses all sense of identity in community loses with it the very marrow of his existence.

The traditions of the Exodus people reflect the early culticizing of that event, celebrated regularly in the rhythm of the year and given form and words, no doubt in extended formulation, but preserved in capsule form in Deuteronomy:

[6] Robert Theobald, *An Alternative Future for America* (Chicago: Swallow Press, 1968), 52.

A wandering Aramean was my father; and he went down into Egypt and sojourned there, few in number; and there he became a nation, great, mighty, and populous. And the Egyptians treated us harshly, and afflicted us, and laid upon us hard bondage. Then we cried to the LORD the God of our fathers, and the LORD heard our voice, and saw our affliction, our toil, and our oppression; and the LORD brought us out of Egypt with a mighty hand and an outstretched arm, with great terror, with signs and wonders; and he brought us into this place and gave us this land, . . . (Deut. 26:5–9)[7]

The rather astonishing vitality of some college and university chapels in a time when would-be prophets are proclaiming the death of corporate worship is surely in part attributable to the fact that it may be the only true celebration of the life and meaning of the community.

Or consider, only for example, what is lost when a couple goes alone to the justice of the peace. This change in life style, this transition of being, this ultimate declaration of love, this consummation of commitment, this momentous, moving human event is presided over, in alien, unfelicitous quarters, by a secular priest never seen before nor to be seen again, who cannot be expected to give a damn about the mechanical words that give legal sanction to the event. Excluded, and impoverished and diminished by the

[7] Compare the form of the same essential cultic confession celebration in Deut. 6:20–24 and, in more extended form, in Joshua 24:2–13.

exclusion, are those who would bring their own love, in all its unfathomable, mysterious, wonderful forms, to celebration if there were celebration. And the lovers are deprived for a lifetime of an enduring human sustenance without which a community even of two is deprived of fullness.

What a difference:

> Dearly beloved—all of us here bound to some of us here in the term 'beloved'—we are gathered together in the sight of God, in the face of this company and in the midst of a troubled world to join together this man and this woman in holy matrimony . . .
> I John, take thee Mary—in the sight of God and in the face of this company of our beloved—to be my wedded wife; to have and to hold from this day forward. . . .
> With this ring I thee wed; this gold I give thee; with my body I thee worship, and with all my worldly goods I thee endow . . . in the sight of God and in the face of this company of the beloved.

Celebration. "Fourscore and seven years ago our forefathers brought forth on this continent a new nation, conceived in liberty, and dedicated to the proposition that all men are created equal." Celebration. "Now thank we all our God, with heart and hands and voices." Celebration. "This child, dearly beloved, is now received into this congregation, into this community of the Church." Celebration. "Mary, dearly beloved, unto God's gracious keeping we commit you." Celebration.

The forms may change. Or we may continue to put, where appropriate, new content and meaning in the old forms. But we must learn afresh how to celebrate, for it is in celebration that we are transformed, renewed, given a heart of flesh, and made a new people, a new creation.

We need a new land, a renewed campus community; we need a new race, a new people, a renewed heart, the recovery of sympathy and perception and corporate celebration. Man in this fractured world also needs new ways of communication and understanding. If we need in any sense a new land and a new race, it is clear also that we desperately need a new language.

Chapter IV

BIBLICAL FOREWORD

But Moses said to God, "Who am I that I should go to Pharaoh, and bring the sons of Israel out of Egypt?" He said, "But I will be with you. . . ." (Exod. 3:11–12)

Then Moses said to God, "If I come to the people of Israel and say to them, 'The God of your fathers has sent me to you, and they ask me, 'What is his name?' what shall I say to them?" God said, "I AM WHO I AM. . . . Say this to the people of Israel, 'I AM has sent me to you.' " (Exod. 3:13–15)

Then Moses answered, "But behold, they will not believe me . . .". (Exod. 4:1)

This is Moses' third protest, and in effect he is asking to be further persuaded. God asks, "What is that in your hand?" Moses says, "A staff." At God's command Moses throws his staff on the ground and it turns into a serpent. But when, at the command of the Word, he catches it, it becomes a staff again. He is told to put his hand under his clothes against his chest. When he draws it out, it is covered with leprosy. At the command of the Word the gesture is repeated and his hand is restored. Finally, water which he takes from the river turns to blood when he pours it out on the ground. The saga does not tell us so, but the parallel inference is clear: at the command of the Word, spilled blood can be turned back to fresh water, death can be turned again to life. (After Exod. 4:1–9)

But Moses said to the Lord, "Oh, my Lord, I am not eloquent, either heretofore or since thou has spoken to thy servant; but I am slow of speech and tongue." Then the Lord said to him, "Who has made man's mouth? Who makes him dumb, or deaf, or seeing, or blind? Is it not I, the Lord? Now therefore go, and I will be with your mouth and teach you what you shall speak." (Exod. 4:10–12)

A NEW LANGUAGE:
The Human Family

*I*т is the novelist John Fowles who supplies us with the titles for these chapters through the words of the young adventurer Nicholas. Taking modest liberties with his statement, we have been reading it in this way: "We don't know where we're going, but we know what we need. We need a new land, a new people, a new language; and although we will have difficulty putting it into words, we need a new mystery." It is the apostle Paul who gives us the overall title and theme in the very personal word he writes to the new Christians in Galatia: "Circumcision is nothing. Uncircumcision is nothing. The only thing that counts is new creation!" The course of the discussion is significantly shaped by ancient stories, worn smooth and timeless and universal by sustained handling in common corporate memory, especially those stories of Abraham and the Exodus. My whole effort is always and everywhere bound and sustained in my lifelong commitment to the company of the Old Testament prophets.

The old structures that in the past have given support and meaning to the life of this nation have become inhibiting of excitement and celebration, of the exercise of responsibility, and of the discovery of self and the other. We need a new land. The old schemes or even the old arguments against them are nothing. All that matters is new creation. Our life is set in the midst of a people whose gifts and powers to live creatively, humanely, and in authentic freedom are diminished and repressed in a kind of latter-day Pharaohism. We need a new race—a renewed people who will be themselves a new creation.

I

And we need a new language. In the world we need a new language. How can we find new language for the United States and Cuba . . . Guatemala . . . Greece . . . Vietnam? How can there be a new creation in language in the Middle East . . . among African states . . . in the politics of the United States, Soviet Russia, Communist China; a new language with and for the multitudes of the subhumanized, humanly diminished by starvation or poverty or color or caste, from Sydney to Bombay to Capetown to Madrid to Jackson and Memphis and Appalachia and Jersey City and Detroit and Chicago? New Language! All that matters is new language—new creation in communication, in understanding, in humanization, in responsibility!

There is an inexpressible, wordless urgency in the whole human situation of chaos. Acts of new creation must be immediately performed if again, as in the primeval myth, the darkness of the deep is to be dissipated; if there is to be light again; if the elements of creation are to be declared "good"; if man is in any sense whatsoever to assume the image of God; if the breath of life, and not of death, is to be in his nostrils. And it is we, above all, we of the great contemporary campus and church family, who must find the way and the words—and the Word, "Let there be light!"— that spoken and enacted produces the content of the word, so that *there is light*, and warmth and response, and understanding and humanity and responsibility.

If we are called out of the campus family and out of the church family to the creation of a new people, we are ultimately charged with the creation of a new language for a new world. The sagas of the patriarchs repeat five times the ultimate meaning of the life of special calling—that in you, through you, by your participation in the human enterprise, all the families

of the earth may be blessed.[1] Implicit if not explicit
in the tales of the Exodus and pointedly stated in the
role of Moses is the sentiment that achieved this particular formulation only centuries later in the Second
Isaiah: It is too inconsequential a matter that you
should be my servant simply for the sake of your own
people: "I will make you the light of the nations so
that my salvation may reach to the ends of the earth."
(Isa. 49:6, JB)

The authoritative word will come to us in different
ways, obviously. Many of university age both on the
campus and in the church are for the moment a-
theological. But what my generation tends to miss in
them—I mean fails to see—is that they are also, for
the most part and in broad definition, profoundly
religious in the sense that large numbers of them are
prepared to be committed to ultimate, authentic
values in a degree and passion not true of my generation or, for that matter, any of the generations between us. They know this Word that comes with
power, and even in a nontheological sense, they understand that we have to spell it with a capital W.

The Moses saga gives it to us in highly personal
terms: Yahweh and Moses have it out with each

[1] In Genesis 12:3, 18:18, and 28:14, the form of the
Hebrew verb permits either a passive ("be blessed") or reflexive ("bless themselves") reading. In two other occurrences
of the covenant promise of universal blessing, 22:15–18 and
26:2–5, the verb form requires the reflexive. From a theological point of view, the distinction is immaterial.

other through four vigorous objections from Moses which in sum border on the insolent and say, in so many words, "Leave me alone, damn it. Let me play my own games in my own ways."

The objections, then and now, *are* intensely personal. The first: Why me? Who am I to make it a new land, help create a new people, and impose a new language on a chaotic world, a world turned back to Babel? The biblical answer is simple—but then so is the corresponding present secular word. Yahweh says to Moses, in effect, "You must define yourself in terms of me. I will be with you. You are God-with-you." Let God be read as God will be read. The sense is clear. In the university and the church, a secular and a theological "Godness" has been given us—in unprecedented, unparalleled measure.

The second protest follows from the first. If I am to identify myself in terms of You, then Who are You? Tell me your Name, by which I will have some notion of your Essence and of what essentially You are! The biblical answer to the second protest provides the stuff of scholars' tomes. But to bypass the technical discussion, the call to fully responsible engagement comes from the eternal I AM (WHO I AM), or I WILL BE (WHAT I WILL BE), or I CAUSE TO BE (all that is in existence). I AM will do, then and now. It is the essence of the nature of being that calls, and if it would exact a commitment to new creation, it conveys, in what it is that calls, a sure promise of ultimate outcome.

"Okay," we and Moses say, "but who's going to believe that the work of new creation is undertaken with the authority of authentic existence itself, at the command of the Lord of Justice, Humanity, and Responsibility?" Comes the perennial response, "If they won't believe you, show them the wonders of man, his ugly miracles by which he makes instruments of death out of structures of support, human disease out of human wholeness, and bloody death out of the water of life. Then show them the wonders of the Word of creation, and persuade them that we, you and I and believing men and women together, can revise the old destructive human magic:

> We can effect the counter miracle.
> The venomous, unleashed, can be contained
> in structures that support the life of man.
> The programmed, calculated brokenness
> of man can be restored, his health returned.
> And we can turn the tide of death to life.[2]

The last protest: I am inarticulate, I am really not qualified. The answer, always adequate with a little faith, even secular faith—I AM, I WILL BE, I CAUSE TO BE, is on your side. What do you want, for God's sake?

[2] B. D. Napier, *Time of Burning* (Philadelphia: United Church Press, 1970), 29.

II

What is required for the creation of a new language? How shall we shape and form a new language for a new world? What will make up the fabric of the redemptive, transforming, creative words, and ultimately the efficacious, self-performing Word calling light out of dark, order out of chaos, life out of death, Israel out of Egypt, freedom out of bondage, and the fulfillment of humanity out of the present widespread human degradation, dereliction, and frustration?

The late H. Richard Niebuhr was my teacher at the Yale Divinity School and later, when I joined that faculty, he was a cherished senior colleague for thirteen years. His last book, published posthumuously in 1963, was called *The Responsible Self.* As a teacher of theology and ethics, Niebuhr's central theme was the ethics of responsibility. In *The Responsible Self,* it is his thesis that in very fact human conduct tends largely to be shaped by an ethics of response. "What is implicit in the idea of responsibility is the image of man-the-answerer, man engaged in dialogue, man acting in response to action upon him." There also exists man the maker, whose ethics is teleological; that is, he asks, "What is my end?" What is good is determined by his goal, his ideal, his telos. For man the citizen it is deontology: What is the law, and what is my ultimate law? For man the responder, for responsible man, the primary ethical question is, What, in this situation to which I must respond, is the appropriate action, the fitting response? As Niebuhr says, "The three approaches may be indicated in the terms, the *good*, the *right*, and the *fitting;* for teleology is concerned always with the highest good to which it subordinates the right; consistent deontology is concerned with the right, no matter what may happen to our goods; but for the ethics of responsibility the *fitting* action, the one that fits into a total interaction as response and as anticipation of further response, is alone conducive to the good and alone is right." [3]

We can all illustrate from our own experience, and out of our own perspectives, the possibly abusive and humanly catastrophic consequences of the systems of the good and the right. If we may, for the sake of emphasis, oversimplify the matter, it may be argued that some of the most destructive effects of nationalism result from the pursuit of a kind of teleological ethics. In the ethical language of departments of state, the ultimate good is the good of the country—not necessarily of all its people but, willy-nilly, of the national entity. Very large numbers of us in this country, and an overwhelming majority of the literate people of the world, regard the pursuit of this good by the United States in Southeast Asia or in Greece and Guatemala as in its total effect thoroughly evil. Given what we claim to be, given the dream behind the

[3] H. Richard Niebuhr, *The Responsible Self* (New York: Harper and Row, 1963), 60.

American reality, the best, highest hopes that have sustained our corporate life as a people; given human aspirations for freedom, self-determination, the human qualities of integrity, compassion, the possibilities of cleanness and gentleness; given the vision of man in the image of God and the sons and daughters of man as brothers and sisters—given all of this, what, in these situations where we act teleologically, would be the fitting action, appropriate to all this that we are or would be and to all that they are and might be?

In these days, one is fed to the teeth with certain extreme forms of a kind of national and international deontology. What is the right can be monumentally wrong; what is the law, ultimately destructive; and what is legal, humanly inequitable and fundamentally unjust. There are those who, with consummate powers of rational legalese, would persuade us that the law and all that comprises the law has dealt appropriately with the Black Panthers and, in courts all too often presided over by judges who, as clergymen or professors, would long since have been retired, has fulfilled itself with justification, given the nature of protests and protestors. But if the system of law—we cannot call it the system of justice—in dealing with the likes of Bobby Seale and Eldridge Cleaver, and the Chicago Seven and their lawyers, and David Harris and Dr. Spock and the Fathers Berrigan and Chaplain Coffin knows only the threat or the act of putting them behind bars, then the right, as right as it may appear from the standpoint of the law, is wrong, and we clearly have no mechanism as a people for the application of an ethics of responsibility, for the realization of what is fitting action, what is appropriate to "a total interaction as response and as anticipation of further response."

I seem to remember a Man, a physician, who performed an act of healing on a day when such an act, along with a great many other acts, was proscribed by law. There was no question of his unrightness, his defiance and violation of the Law. This was the Palestinian, you remember, who said that "the Sabbath was made for the sake of man and not man for the Sabbath." (Mark 2:27, NEB.) The Sabbath is nothing; circumcision and uncircumcision are nothing where human values, human life, human fulfillment are at stake. And the prophets in whose company, and even in whose debt, Jesus often found himself, did not respond to the question, What does the Lord require of you; what is the ultimate demand? by saying, "Pursue your own destiny at any cost, and observe the commandments." One said it for all when he said simply, "to act justly, to love tenderly, and to walk humbly with your God." (Micah 6:8, JB) The *responsible* self—an ethics of responsibility!

Niebuhr sees all ethical schemes pressing ultimately to questions of universal implication:

When we approach man's existence . . . with the aid of the idea of responsibility, we are caught up in the same movement toward the universal in which the other approaches to ethics, that is, teleology and deontology, find themselves involved. In teleological ethics we move forward asking as our final question. . . . "What is the Form of the Good that is the form of the whole?" In deontology we eventually ask: "What is the universal form of the law?" And now in the ethics of the fitting, we find ourselves led to the notion of universal responsibility. . . . The responsible self is driven as it were by the movement of the social process to respond and be accountable in nothing less than a universal community.[4]

The new language that we need in a world that desperately needs a new language will be the language of the responsible self, responding ultimately in universal terms—that is, responding to humanity.

I cannot leave Niebuhr without one further observation. In his teaching, always fresh, always marked by signs of his own immediate struggle with the matter at hand, it was not uncommon for him to tell us, after giving us a lecture or two or three, that we would have to demolish that which struck us as surely the final and most eloquent word on the subject. Or he would explain why it could not stand as it was and how we would have either to begin all over again, or to modify it, hedge against its weaknesses, or revise it.

In *The Responsible Self*, having won us as adherents of an ethics of responsibility and indeed, I think, hav-

[4] *Ibid.*, 87.

ing persuaded the reader that all has been said that could be said, he reminds us that this system and any system is time bound; and that, if there is no conscious, deliberate defense against it, the response will always be fettered, controlled, dictated by traditional modes of memory of the past and expectations of the future. "Man responding in the present is interpreting what acts upon him as historical being, being in time." And this means, in *our* time, that "our actual ethics, personal and social, is to a large extent analyzable as defense ethics or as ethics of survival." [5] And he continues: "It is characteristic of our age that we come to each particular occasion with the understanding that the world is full of enemies though it contains some friends. Hence, we respond to all actions upon us with an evaluatory scheme: beings are either good or evil; they belong to the class of things that ought to be or those that ought not to be. And ultimately the distinction between them has to be made by reference to the way they support or deny our life." [6] I take Niebuhr to be saying, although he does not say it this way, that in our time it is a *world* that lives in anxiety and fear and that we are all haunted by the specter of death, not simply physical death, although that too, but death in the sense of the loss of that without which we deem life to be worthless and without meaning.

If this is the prevailing response, if the responsible

[5] *Ibid.*, 98.
[6] *Ibid.*, 99.

ethic, at all levels, is in fact ethics of defense and survival; if we act, in other words, by mechanisms of response imposed by the inherited, traditional, culturally accommodated interpretation of all three of our tenses, past, present, and future, then our situation is quite without hope. Our language remains the destructive language of Babel and no new language will be forthcoming. "And so, when we analyze ourselves as responsive, time-full beings the question of freedom arises . . . the question of the self's ability in its present to change its past and future and to achieve or receive a new understanding of its ultimate historical context. If [this is] possible, then reinterpretation of present action upon the self must result, and a new kind of reaction, a response that fits into another lifetime and another history, can and will take place." [7]

Therefore, I turn now to all of us who make up the vast American college and church company. If we are called, as we are to be sure, in different ways, to the now absolutely critical leadership of a universal people, *we* must create a new language of responsibility because it may well be we alone can. We must produce a fresh response, redemptive words, nondefensive, nonsurvival words, *the* Word, a whole new language that "fits right now into another lifetime and another history" to give us all a productive life

[7] *Ibid.*, 101.

and a fulfilled history. It is a matter of fact, and one of enormous hope, that increasing numbers of students in this generation are already insisting on a language appropriate to another lifetime and another history, a new history, a new creation.

III

We need a new language of responsibility. We also need a new language of man. The course of theology in this century has not greatly helped us. I grew up in fundamentalism. I have said earlier that my parents were missionaries in China, where I was born and reared through two years of high school. Man was an unqualified stinker but you could remove the stench by baptism—for me that meant immersion and we did not heat the water—and by praying and singing hymns and spending (it seemed to me) half your life in the company of other baptized, praying, singing, deodorized stinkers. And for this you could go to heaven. All of this was knocked out of me when I went to a liberal seminary and learned that there were some pretty grim things going on out there that could be ungrimmed (so it seemed to me they were teaching us) if we enlightened liberals would just have at it together. Who needed God? We would crack a few heads, change a few laws, and, presto, a new land, a new race, and a new language! At one time I believed that if all the agencies of government could be turned over to the faculty of the Yale Divinity

School, the Kingdom of God on earth would be ushered in within a single administration. That was, of course, before I became a member of that faculty.

This prideful, idolatrous but ardent faith gave way, when I began teaching, to what appears in retrospect to have been a kind of neofundamentalism. It was not bound, like the old fundamentalism, to a literalist reading of scripture, in which every word is the unqualified utterance of God; but, under the stern aegis of Karl Barth; haunted by the revived ghost of the dour Dane, Kierkegaard; fed by the prestigious, modish, secular eixstentialism of Jaspers and Heidegger; and given "orthodox" standing in Protestant theology by Bultmann and Tillich, this new fundamentalism, or new orthodoxy, returned a description of man in some respects even more depressing than that of fundamentalism. Now I am not for a moment trying to suggest that all these men were, to use the vernacular, in the same bag. Indeed, some of their disciples would be indignant at their coming together in the same paragraph. However, what was impressed upon lesser men, would-be followers in their train, by this superb array of theological and philosophical talent was an image of man, on his own devices, hopelessly crippled, tragically bound in his finiteness, inextricably caught in his sense of anxiety and guilt, faced always with the frailty and ultimate collapse of all his own structures of meaning and security, and living, of necessity, only toward death. And in some formulations of the Christian gospel in this view of miserable man, it was precisely the point that the saving grace of God in Christ could reach him only when and as he wallowed in his worthlessness.

Now we see in some younger theologians a reaction to this which, in the typical nature of re-action, sometimes swings too wide and too far in the other direction. Dietrich Bonhoeffer, German martyr executed by Hitler for his part in the plot against the dictator's life, would appear to be the specific agent of turning. If we are witnessing thesis and antithesis, the synthesis is not yet clear. What is clear is that the theological, and I think the secular, language of man is changing. The language *about* man, descriptive of man, may already be on the way to becoming a new language. It is not at all that we repudiate our affection or admiration or appreciation for the likes of Sartre and Camus on the one hand, or, on the other, our continuing indebtedness to a preceding generation of philosophers and theologians. Indeed, the very shaping of the new language is given impetus by their own involvement in and interpretation of human finitude and anguish. It would be inconceivable without their work and remains properly subject to their discipline and restraint.

But a new language about man is fast emerging, and what he becomes depends in part on his *name*, what in essence he understands himself to be apart from what he says of himself, what he calls himself, what his self-language is. He possesses now, for the first time in his history, the power to destroy himself or, by the same kinds of power, to redeem himself in his human family from the besetting ills of all his time.

The grammar for the new language of man has not been written but, I think, is being written; and a large part of the work is being done, will have to be done, by the only two establishments qualified to do it— the university and the church. We cannot now be sure that we speak the new language but we must try. It is easier, by pointing to the two extremes, to say what it is not. This, spoken by a Nobel Prize winner in biology, is hardly the new language.

> Science can afford men ever newer horizons and higher peaks to climb, materially, mentally, and spiritually . . . its pathway leads not only outward into space and to other worlds than ours, but also inward into the recesses of life, of the mind, and of the heart. By its means we will ourselves assume the role of creators of ever lovelier worlds and of more sublime beings. By its means too, we can reach increasing agreement regarding the nature of things, since the conclusions of science rest on objective tests. . . . Thus will the beast in man transcend himself, and the sublime burst forth in a mounting symphony of self-creation.[8]

The antidote to this—which could be called the

[8] Herman J. Muller, "The Uses of Tolerance," in *Saturday Review*, February 13, 1965.

fable of Man and Science—is the much older fable of
the scorpion and the turtle, or man and his existence.
It goes like this:

> The scorpion, being a very poor swimmer, asked the
> turtle to carry him across the river on his back. "Are you
> mad?" asked the turtle. "You'll sting me while I'm
> swimming and I'll drown."
>
> "My dear turtle," laughed the scorpion, "if I were to
> sting you, you would drown and I would go down with
> you. Now what's the logic in that?"
>
> "You're right," cried the turtle, "hop on." The scorpion
> climbed aboard and halfway across the river gave the
> turtle a mighty sting. As they both sank to the bottom,
> the turtle said with a quiet resignation, "Do you mind
> if I ask you something? You said there'd be no logic in
> your stinging me. Why did you do it?" The drowning
> scorpion sadly replied, "It has nothing to do with logic.
> It's just my nature."

The new language of man will be disciplined and
informed by both of these extremes, but it will not
be the language of either of these fables, the language
of instrumental redemption or of human despair. The
new language of man will emphasize his deeds as
maker and doer, his new potential as creature, his gifts
of imagination and ingenuity; but it will be articulate
about his heart, and it will be sensitive and eloquent
in describing the difference between a heart of stone
and a heart of flesh, between circumcision and a new

creation. It will be realistically hopeful about the hazards of lethal power in the body and mind of the sometimes scorpion and it will dare to use all meaningful formulations of utopia; it will be informed and self-conscious about the uses of utopia.

A younger American theologian, himself struggling to find the new language of responsibility and a new language of man, is, I think, speaking the language when he says to would-be Christians: "What is needed is an understanding of the Christian gospel that will illumine the meaning of man's power and will enable him to exercise that power in authentically human ways for authentically human ends. A theology which obscures the urgency of this challenge or encourages flight from it is not simply irresponsible; it is positively demonic!" [9]

We need a new language of mutual human responsibility. We need a new language of man for what must be a new world.

IV

We also need a new language of utopia, a utopia that will never *be* the new world but that will alone enable us to see the old world for what it is, and that will be the image for the transformation of the old into a new creation.

[9] Thomas W. Ogletree, "From Anxiety to Responsibility: The Shifting Focus of Theological Reflection," in *Chicago Theological Seminary Register*, LVIII (March, 1968), 13.

I suppose man has always put human labels to
pernicious use. I want to say something about Karl
Marx and Herbert Marcuse; and I suppse I ought to
round out the trinity with some appropriate quotation from Chairman Mao. On an earlier page I quoted
Berthhold Brecht, who was a Marxist. He was also a
man—a man of rare sensitivity and insight and human
compassion. I suppose Marx was a Marxist, although
one wonders about that in the same way one wonders
whether Christ was a Christian. Incidentally, another
point of similarity between Marxism and the biblical
faiths is unintentionally expressed by a Marx biog-
rapher who says of the Marxist Bible *Das Kapital*
that it was "not so much widely read as revered." [10]

Old Karl Marx—also very much a man, with a kind
of uncompromising integrity that over and over again
almost ruined him—shook and still shakes the founda-
tions of the human exploiters of men in part by the
language of utopia. You can keep men in hell if they
have no vision of anything better; and certainly it is
easier to maintain acceptance of any status quo when
there is no articulate dream of a better human world.
People will stay with a diet of leeks, onion, and garlic
until they hear of a land flowing with milk and honey.

Conservative elements, especially in southern California, have given Professor Marcuse and the administration at the University of California in San Diego

[10] Helene Lecar, *Karl Marx: A Concise Biography* (New
York: American R.D.M. Corp., 1966), 51.

a lot of trouble over his writings and his brilliant, exciting teaching. If the use of appropriate, corresponding utopias by which alone we are enabled to see that our unrealized potential is dangerous, then to be sure Marcuse is dangerous.[11]

And the students who speak and act for change and reform are dangerous. As one commentary on the Columbia incident put it, some of the "students were unashamedly old-fashioned enough to offer up a utopian vision of social institutions that do not need to defend their values by repression. The students made the great refusal; they were romantic; they dreamed the impossible." [12]

Jesus was dangerous—his utopia was nothing less than the Kingdom of God. And how do we see ourselves now, over against that kind of vision? The prophets were dangerous: by what utopias they betrayed the violence and harshness of their status quo and the universal status quo! Here is a world where the bitterest, most violently sustained international enmity is erased: "In that day [in this utopia] there will be a highway from Egypt to Assyria, and the Assyrian will come into Egypt, and the Egyptian into Assyria, and the Egyptians will worship with the Assyrians . . . Israel will be the third with Egypt and

[11] I strongly recommend the reading of Marcuse's *One-Dimensional Man* (Boston: Beacon Press, 1964).
[12] "The Siege of Columbia," in *Ramparts* (June, 1968), 26–39.

Assyria, a blessing in the midst of the earth. . . ." (Isa. 19:23–25) Or a new land, a new people, a new language: "The wolf shall dwell with the lamb, and the leopard shall lie down with the kid, and the calf and the lion and the fatling together, and a little child shall lead them." (Isa. 11:6) And that classical prophetic utopia which refuses to fall into silence: "[Men] shall beat their swords into plowshares, and their spears into pruning hooks; nation shall not lift up sword against nation, neither shall they learn war any more; but they shall sit every man under his vine and under his fig tree, and none shall make them afraid; for the mouth of the LORD of hosts has spoken." (Micah 4:3–4)

New language, new words, and the Word. And we are back again to Moses, who gave classical form to the utopias of every subsequent Exodus, every human venture toward new creation. He gave it in the promise of a land, a new world, flowing with milk and honey. It was not and it is not that. It could not be and it cannot be that; but without the promise, the vision, the dream, the language of utopia, human enslavement to Pharaohism is never broken and a new language, a new history, and a new creation remain forever unattainable.

Chapter V

BIBLICAL FOREWORD

When all things began, the Word already was . . . ; no single thing was created without him. (John 1:1-3, NEB)

In the beginning . . . God *said*, "Let there be light"; and there was light. (Gen. 1:1-3)

My word . . . shall not return to me empty, but it shall accomplish that which I purpose, and prosper in the thing for which I sent it. (Isa. 55:11)

I am God and not man, the Holy One in your midst. . . . (Hosea 11:9)

So the Word became flesh; he came to dwell among us, and we saw his glory, such glory as befits the Father's only Son, full of grace and truth. (John 1:14, NEB)

We . . . bring you good news that you should turn from these vain things to a living God who made the heaven and the earth and the sea and all that is in them. . . . [and] he [has not left] himself without witness [anywhere!]. (Acts 14:15-17)

They are a rebellious people, lying sons, sons who will not hear the instruction of the Lord; who say to the seers, "See not"; and to the prophets, "Prophesy not to us what is right; speak to us smooth things, prophesy illusions . . . let us hear no more of the Holy One of Israel." (Isa. 30:9-11)

[Jesus said] whoever would save his life will lose it; and whoever loses his life for my sake, he will save it. (Luke 9:24) In truth, in very truth I tell you, a grain of wheat remains a solitary grain unless it falls into the ground and dies; but if it dies, it bears a rich harvest. (John 12:24, NEB)

Behold the servant of God who bears all human grief and carries all human sorrow, who is himself wounded for the transgressions of men and bruised for their iniquities; and whose stripes are for the healing of the families of the earth (Isa. 53:4–5, adapted).

For you who fear my name the sun of righteousness shall rise, with healing in its wings. You shall go forth leaping like calves from the stall. (Malachi 4:2)

A NEW MYSTERY: *The Church*

WE do not know where we are going, but we know what we need. We need a new land, a new race, a new language; and although we cannot really put it into words, we need a new mystery.

For a long time now, beginning certainly in the 1930's, we of the broad company of biblically oriented believers have been discarding baggage no longer pertinent to the needs of our journey; and in the decade just past we have been tossing it overboard—with what has appeared to some in our great family as heedless abandon. We have not only de-mythologized our faith; we have, to an extent never dreamed of in our history, also de-mysterized it as well. Our faith supports little wonder. Our unfaith is aggressively intolerant of mystery. What may be the ultimate consequences, one cannot predict. No one wants useless cargo aboard; but we were surely chartered to preserve for ourselves and to carry to our ports of call a mystery that is quite unashamedly out of this world. It is of our essence and if we have lost it, if we have let it go, if we have abandoned it, we are undone and we will perish for want of fulfillment.

Some, especially in the universities, are persuaded that we are without a viable mystery, and they are looking elsewhere for the mystery without which neither they nor any man can live. They are looking in unprecedented numbers and fervor for a new mystery—some in sex, some (I think, on the campus in diminishing numbers) in drugs, many in astrology or spiritualism or both, or in one or even several of the mushrooming sects of eastern religions; and still others are answering the hunger for mystery somewhere in the astonishing proliferation of the T-group, the encounter seminar in which mysterious and heretofore untouched depths of the *person* are exposed and probed.

Biblical people, whether Jews or Christians, exist as keepers of a mystery. It is right that old forms, no longer cogent, be discarded. But the essential mystery, the biblical mystery, must be re-appropriated, re-formed, re-created into a new and compelling and sustaining mystery by which we may live and out of which we may create the stuff of a new history.

I

The church is the keeper of the mystery of the Word. The church is the custodian, the proclaimer, *and the doer* of the Word—or it is not the church. Aware of the mystery of the Word and the wonder of the Word, the church, which is the total body of Christ's believers, must have knowledge among its members of the scope of the Word, the sometimes whimsy of the Word, or its unobtrusiveness, certainly the masquerades of the Word. And so it must not be afraid to identify the Word, however incongruous the circumstances of its appearing, and to interpret the Word, however devastating even to its own members, or however seemingly incredible or absurd or naïve it may seem to any man, within or without the church. For this is part of the mystery of the Word.

At the same time, the church must know that it is never itself the Word nor does it *possess* the Word. The Word was from the beginning and will be, world without end. If the church were not, the Word would be. God has not and will not leave Himself without witness *anywhere*. But the church cannot live if the mystery of the Word is lost.

One of the oldest forms maintained without interruption in the long life of biblical faith is preaching. It is of the very essence of preaching that it is undertaken in the hope and even the expectation that it may be invaded by the Word. Preaching knows that it will never possess the Word or command the Word at will. It prays and exists that it may, if only fragmentarily, be possessed by the Word.

This preaching, this ancient struggle involving gathered believers and preacher and Spirit and Word, is now seriously and vigorously attacked *within the church* as a form no longer effective and therefore useless in the practice of the life of faith; and, on what is to me an alarming scale, it is being abandoned to other allegedly more compelling devices for the possibility of the entertainment and interpretation of the mystery of the Word.

Now this is an area in which I have, if not expertise, at least involvement and commitment. My father and brother took clerical orders. My grandfather was a preacher. Seventeen years of my life were spent teaching in a seminary. If preaching is nothing that I have taught, preachers are; and preaching is something I have done all my adult life. I know that a lot of what passes for preaching really does not give the Word a chance; that it is dull and irrelevant; that it is unprophetic or antiprophetic in the sense that it aims precisely at speaking the smooth word, at confirming the comfortable illusion; and that it is in short an exercise in vacuity.

This is not the time and place for the diagnosis and prognosis for Wordless preaching. Critics of the preaching form are absolutely right if in fact, as they allege, preaching fails to "involve" the hearers. But then this is not preaching. It is a homily. It is a twenty-minute lecture. It is a talk.

One of the reasons that I left a teaching post a few years ago for a university chaplaincy was that for years I had been doing what was called preaching, but what failed to be preaching because it was not a transaction involving pulpit and pew, sermon and congregation, proclamation and reception; but was in effect platform and auditorium, religious lecture and audience, speaking and listening. Let me tell you how this looks to me now, this kind of hit-and-run exercise in which I was engaged almost every Sunday in term time for seventeen years.

It is a couple of minutes before eleven on a Sunday morning. The narthex of the school chapel seems to be nearly overflowing with the robed young bodies of the choir. I may have been here to preach the year before and the year before that. I may have been making an annual frantic trip for fifteen years. But I do not recognize any of the faces in the choir nor do I know any of the students in the congregation.

I am also robed—and hooded. As the organist starts the processional hymn I check to be sure the pages of the sermon manuscript are all there, and in order. I recall with still acute dismay an Easter morning in a school pulpit some years before when I reached the conclusion of the sermon and found the last page missing. The chaplain, the headmaster, or the president—whomever I happen to be marching with—

reminds me that I will be sitting on the left side of the chancel; and as I proceed down the center aisle between rows of young strangers, it mercifully does not occur to me that I know nothing concrete about the immediate life of this school. It would appear that I do not want to know. If the school is within driving distance, I left just enough time to make the service without risking cardiac arrest in the chaplain. As I climb the chancel steps, I am praying for the service and the sermon, but at the same time wondering whether there is not some pretext on which I can decline the invitation to lunch and so be on my way home again in an hour or so.

Or, if I have come some distance, I took the latest possible flight last night and arrived much too late to be asked to have breakfast with students. I appeared at the chapel only fifteen minutes before the service. I can stay after chapel only long enough to shake a few hands, because I must be at the airport for a 1:30 flight.

It proves to be a good day; which is to say the sermon goes well; which is to say that I am thanked and praised and that copies of the sermon are requested. The sermon ought to go well. I wrote it first for Yale or Stanford, revised it for Vanderbilt, adapted it for use in a couple of prepschool chapels, and gave it a major refurbishing a couple of weeks ago for Chicago.

But, dearly beloved, the question I have to ask myself in the presence of God and in the face of this company is whether, under these circumstances, I have in fact preached. I have delivered a sermon, there is no question about that. But have I engaged in preaching?

It is not my intention to denounce the role and function of the guest in the pulpit. The visiting fireman, as he is affectionately known on the circuit, can be a highly effective sermonizer. Hit-and-run pulpit speaking (I would rather not call it preaching) can strike a blow for the Kingdom or deftly puncture the pride of the congregation in a way not given to the resident preacher, precisely because the visitor is innocent (or can claim innocence) of the particularities of the life of his people. So far from depreciating the value of the guest sermon, I would urge parish churches, budgets permitting, of course, to run an every fourth or fifth Sunday program inviting for the most part nonparish clergymen from universities and seminaries to speak specifically without regard for the alleged shorn lambs of the parish congregation. I would also urge the opening of pulpits to lay people, pointedly not to theologize but to humanize, to speak out of their own particular professional expertise on the fearful problems that now harass, plague, and destroy the family of man.

But there is surely a difference—no superficial difference, but a difference in essence—between the preaching of stranger to strangers on the one hand,

and on the other, the fashioning and release of words which may, by the grace of God, convey the particular Word to a particular, mutually familiar gathered people, in this particular moment of a life and a time and a place, and even of particular circumstances, that are all shared. I do not for a moment mean to deny the possibility of the presence of the Word in the preaching of the onetime guest in the pulpit or, for that matter, say, in the preaching of a Billy Graham. But that phenomenon of grace which is the intimate Word, for this people, in this moment, is a sheer gift of the Spirit to the community congregation of which the preacher is himself a part; and the Word, if and as it appears, is a mystery made tangible, not alone by the prayers and the words of the preacher, but by his sense of identity with people, his participation in their life *and theirs in his,* and the knowledge and acceptance of all of a common life and a common trust.

Some time ago we had a very distinguished and effective guest in the Stanford pulpit who delivered himself of some remarks to which, on the following Sunday, I responded as follows:

In his sermon last Sunday Dr. so-and-so said something about this pulpit being twenty feet above criticism; and I think he meant to suggest the view, often voiced, that the sermon is a kind of one-way, over-the-head method of communication. It may be that he was saying in a kind way that preaching is for the birds.

The fact was that our pulpit guest, having made his deprecatory remarks about preaching, went on that morning for a lot longer than I ever do. He spoke with deep conviction and with the obvious assurance that he was being heard. And when it was over, he reported that the whole thing was a highly exhilarating and rewarding experience.

My response the following Sunday had its more serious words: "It is precisely the point of a *resident* preacher," I said, "that he is *there*; that he shares the same life; and that what emerges in his own sermons is the product of his own unceasing openness to conversation, to reprimand and criticism, or to support and encouragement. What I say here is always in the nature of response—to you, to this place, to our time, and to all our shared anguish, and perplexity, and joy."

It concerns me now that I did not say what I ought to have said and what I might have said: that while we are here to praise God and celebrate in His light the meaning of our particular life together, it is our hope and expectation that the Word will break forth among us; and that the possibility of this mystery, this act of grace, inheres not in words of mine I speak, but words of *ours*, and comes to reality, if it comes, only *among us*. And I should have said, this mystery is in any case a gift of God.

I once took a seminary course entitled "The Art of Preaching." In a certain sense, the title strikes me now as almost an offense. Of course, artistry is involved in the production and performance of the sermon (to speak again in necessary but, in themselves alone, offensive terms), and the preacher must indeed cultivate the sensitivities, intuitions, and skills of the artist appropriate to his own particular calling and function. But preaching is the total expression of the commitment of the total person to the support of the total life of man, in and through a given community of which he is himself totally a part. And it prays and exists—to say it again—that it may, if even fragmentarily, be possessed by the Word, release the Word, and make tangible once more the grace of the mystery of the Word, in and among this people, my people, of whom I am one.

Where two or three are gathered, or twenty or thirty, or two or three hundred, or a thousand or more, the Word may come in and through the words that are preached; and it is always a part of the mystery of the Word that it is sustaining, renewing, and creative and that it leads always in the direction of a new history.

II

It is, of course, of the character of the mystery of the Word that it comes—emphatically not only in preaching or under some other church auspices, but in improbable and unsuspected ways—under circumstances which would in themselves appear to deny the possibility of the presence of the Word, and even to

men and women who are persuaded that such a
mystery as the Word cannot be. But if the church,
which is the people of faith, is the custodian and
keeper of the Word, it must be open to the seeming
promiscuity of the Word, as it were, its capriciousness,
its independence, its stubbornness to go its own way.
And faith, standing open and sensitive to the whole
range of existence, must trust the gift of a kind of
extrasensory perception of the Word, which is also
a part of its mystery. The life of faith, standing always
so, and trusting so, will identify the Word, embrace
the Word, interpret the Word, and appropriate the
Word to the purposes of a new creation.

My colleague Robert McAfee Brown, writing in
the beginning of this decade on the changes in his
own perspectives during the sixties, speaks also for
me when he says:

> Ten years ago I had pretty well worked out my own
> understanding of the gospel, and I saw my task as one
> of finding ways to communicate that gospel to those
> around me. Now I see much more clearly that the traffic
> between the gospel and the world travels a two-way
> street. The gospel helps to inform and define the world,
> but *the world helps to inform and define the gospel*. . . .
> I have come to believe very much in "the pseudonyms
> of God" . . . that God is at work in an infinitely wider
> arena of activities than I had earlier believed. . . . It is
> out of the stuff of human life and experience that we

get the pointers and hints to suggest, however faintly, something of the reality of the divine.[1]

Something of the same thing is expressed in these lines descriptive of the Word and, after the manner of the Old Testament prophet, put in the formula, "Thus says Yahweh":

> I cannot go beyond my Word—the soft
> persistent Word, the Word that I have spoken
> from time to time to some who know I speak
> and some who do not know, but hear and speak
> the Word again, unlabeled; paint the Word
> or write the Word or act the Word unmarked
> and unidentified, but still the Word . . . .
> the Word that always *is*, however much
> men try to say "it was" or "it shall be"! [2]

This is the Word. It is totally among us, among us all. It comes *only* "among us" and the church will never know its full mystery if the church lives only in the church. It is a part of the mystery of the Word that it may come as well where it is denied as where it is affirmed; that it is to be known less where there is order than where there is chaos, comfort than anguish, living then dying. For it is a part of the mystery of the Word that it comes with healing on its wings, to revive, to restore, to create anew.

[1] Robert McAfee Brown, "Discoveries and Dangers," in *Christian Century*, January 14, 1970.
[2] B. D. Napier, *Come Sweet Death* (Philadelphia: United Church Press, 1967), 61.

III

We need a new mystery for a new history, for a
new creation. We will find it, and we must, in a new,
immediate, uninhibited apropriation of the Word—
to be sure *in the church,* and even and emphatically
in the preaching of those of us who undertake it with
self-doubt and fear and uncertainty, but as well where
the possibility of the Word is seemingly denied. And
the church, while never the sole recipient of the Word,
remains the Word's custodian and keeper and proclaimer, in the sense that the people of faith alone
may be able to recognize and embrace and prophesy
and celebrate the Word in its utterly unidentified
and seemingly arbitrary explosions into being.

It may be, too—in this age when more of us are
more conscious than we have ever been before of
man's incredible capacity for the making of death,
the creation of death as it were—that in death itself
there is a new mystery, a mystery like the Word and
akin to the Word, that is also in the peculiar keeping
of the church.

To speak of the making and manipulation of death,
the grotesque, macabre celebration and deification of
death which now characterizes and preoccupies the
powerful nation-states under our sun, is to bring to
mind that scene in the Great Hall of the University
of Salamanca late in the year 1936, when the Rector
of the University spat in the teeth of Franco's proud
purveyors of death.

His name was Miguel de Unamuno; he was, of course, presiding. Señora Franco was on the platform, with other dignitaries and leaders in Franco's Nationalist party. The speaker was General Millán Astray, whose theme was that fascism would bring health to Spain by death; and several times, to cries of approval from the Falangists in the audience, he shouted his motto, "*Viva la Muerte!*"

Unamuno's response surely marks one of the high points in the history of the human race. In part he said:

> At times to be silent is to lie. For silence can be interpreted as acquiescence. . . . Just now I heard a necrophilous and senseless cry: "Long live death!" And I, who have spent my life shaping paradoxes which have aroused the uncomprehending anger of others, I must tell you, as an expert authority, that this outlandish paradox is repellent to me. General Millán Astray is a cripple. Let it be said without any slighting undertone. He is a war invalid. So was Cervantes. . . . It pains me to think that General Millán Astray should dictate the pattern of mass psychology. A cripple who lacks the spiritual greatness of Cervantes is wont to seek ominous relief in causing mutilation around him.[3]

General Astray could take this no more. He inter-

[3] Hugh Thomas, *The Spanish Civil War* (New York: Harper and Row, 1961), 354. And see James Michener's account and his affirmation of the essential historical accuracy of the same dramatic scene in Michener, *Iberia* (New York: Fawcett, 1969), 539 ff.

rupted Unamuno with a shout, *"Abajo la Inteligencia!*
Viva la Muerte!" When the general's supporters were
quiet again, Unamuno went on: "This is the temple
of the intellect, and I am its high priest. It is you who
profane its sacred precincts. You will win, because
you have more than enough brute force. But you will
not convince." And Unamuno finished by saying
simply, "I have done." He lost his freedom immediately, and he died within a matter of weeks.

There is no mystery but only madness in this kind
of praise of death, and the university and the church
must oppose it, wherever it occurs and by whomever
it is celebrated and perpetrated. The Word in the
midst of the calculated creation of death is surely its
holy, eternal, passionate, and absolute repudiation!
And we, both in the university and the church, must
speak now where our silence may be interpreted as
acquiescence. Our own psychological, death-manu-
facturing cripples have got to be cared for in other
ways than housing them in offices of power in government and the Pentagon.

But there is death that is not a part of any human
scheme, death that comes to us all—that is, if we
avoid the still-expanding network of devices for in-
flicting death that become programmed either by
intention or by heedlessness and greed. Our present
increasing awareness of and repugnance toward anything that smacks of the cry *"Viva la Muerte!"* may
help us in the appropriation of the mystery of death

that is creative, that brings new things, new life, and even a new history.

It is not, as we know, a new mystery. It was sounded in the Isaianic Servant Songs more than twenty-five hundred years ago; it is a flat statement of the Gospel—he that would save his life must lose it; and the whole event of Jesus Christ is reduced to nonsense apart from the mystery of creative death. And yet, a new mystery it must become, because we have lost the old mystery. What a gruesome and reprehensible contradiction we are caught in today in our culture! On the one hand, for all our apparent and increasing sensitivity, we join in very fact in the cry of Millán Astray, "*Viva la Muerte*": we contribute, all of us, rather incessantly these days, to any of a number of sustained and established forms of living death in the effects of our abuse of power (in what subtle ways is it given to us to kill!); our racism (by act or acquiescence); our pollution, our rape of our physical environment (we talk, but what do we do?); and above all, our quite apparent complacency in living on the fat of the land when the majority of our fellows sharing our time and our planet are in fact in an existence better described by death than life. And this is to say nothing of our direct participation in dying death, death that is literal death.

I speak of a contradiction. At the same time, we are, as a culture, assiduously and expensively engaged in deceiving ourselves and our immediate fellows about our own inexorable dying. We choose to masque with skill and ingenuity both the process and the fact. The university lends its resources in varied ways to this infantile masquerade. The church—may God forgive us and bring us again into the ways of truth and faith!

If we are to reappropriate the mystery of death, if we are to know at all the new mystery of creative death, and above all if the church is to fulfill its charge to be the sustainer and proclaimer of the mystery, we cannot participate any longer in deception (and who, my brothers and sisters in the church, does it more adeptly than we?). How close are we to the novelist James Cozzen's description of Helen Detweiler: "On the world she never made, she imposed with all her strength a pattern of the world she wanted—a place of peace, of order, of security; a good and honest world, the abode of gentle people, who . . . once believed into existence, could alleviate [her] recurrent anguish of trying not to know, yet always knowing, that in the midst of life we are in death." [4]

In my reading during recent years, two novels, a collection of memoirs, and an essay stand out in my mind as comprehending and conveying a sense of death as a creative mystery—creative in the sense of pointing to the possibilities of a new history, and

[4] James Gould Cozzens, *By Love Possessed* (New York: Harcourt, Brace, 1957), 39–40.

creative as well in putting life in a fresh perspective of meaning and wonder.

One of these is a novel by the late James Agee called *A Death in the Family* (later skillfully and sensitively adapted to the stage by Tad Mosel under the title *All the Way Home*). The death in the family is that of a young husband and father, and the novel looks with compassion and unfaltering honesty at the tragic event and its consequences in the immediate existence of the survivors, especially that of the young wife. It is her father who warns her, and all of us, against the abuse of faith. He is an agnostic, she, a devout Christian. In those first days of awful grief mitigated by shock, he has the courage to tell her what is true:

> It's bad enough right now, but it's going to take a while to sink in. When it really sinks in it's going to be any amount worse. It'll be so much worse you'll think it's more than you can bear. Or any other human being. And worse than that, you'll have to go through it alone, because there isn't a thing on earth any of us can do to help, beyond blind animal sympathy. . . . It's a kind of test, Mary, and it's the only kind that amounts to anything. When something rotten like this happens. Then you have your choice. You start to really be alive, or you start to die. That's all.

There is a long mutually-sustaining silence between them, and then he goes on: "I imagine you're thinking about your religion. . . . Well, more power to you.

I know you've got a kind of help I could never have. Only one thing: take the greatest care you don't just—crawl into it like a hole and hide in it." [5]

How can we know death as a creative mystery if, by whatever means, we avoid its full confrontation? And if death is disguised or, by some colossal act of deception, rendered innocuous, then life is deprived of the ultimate measure of its poignancy and beauty. In the midst of life we are in death; or, as Luther put it for those who believe, in a sermon on Abraham and Isaac, in the midst of death we are in life. We do not, then, presume fully to separate light and dark, and life and death, and blessing and curse. Above all, we must do nothing to stifle or suppress or distort or minimize or disguise or, by any other device, to dissipate the mystery of the conspiracy of death. To do this would be to render quite unauthentic and empty all joyfulness in the conspiracy of grace. It is a part of the mystery of death that we cannot live with creativity if we disguise death or in some insubstantial formula believe that we have contrived to exorcise it.

A second novel that is, in this sense, redemptive of death is by Peter de Vries. Called *The Blood of the Lamb*, it is the story of his own loss of a young daughter to leukemia. When she is in the hospital for the last time and now in fact dying after several cruel periods of remission, the father goes to a nearby

[5] James Agee, *A Death in the Family* (New York: Mc-Dowell, Obolensky, 1957), 155–56.

church and prays. And some of the simplest mysteries of grace *in life* are given expression in his anguished knowledge of the seeming silence of God, and in the agony of his acceptance of the mystery of death:

> ... give us [another] year [but he knows this may not be]. We will spend it as we have the last, missing nothing. We will mark the dance of every hour between the snowdrop and the snow; crocus to tulip to violet to iris to rose. We will note not only the azalea's crimson flowers but . . . [we] will seek out the leaves turning in the little-praised bushes and the unadvertised trees. . . . We will note the lost yellows in the tangles of that bush that spills over the Howards' stone wall. . . . We will seek out these modest subtleties so lost in the blare of oaks and maples, like flutes and woodwinds drowned in brasses and drums. When winter comes, we will let no snow fall ignored. We will again watch the first blizzard from her window like figures locked snug in a glass paperweight. "Pick one out and follow it to the ground!" she will say again. We will feed the plain birds that stay to cheer us through the winter, and when spring returns we shall be the first out, to catch the snow-drop's first white whisper in the wood. All this we ask, with the remission of our sins, in Christ's name. Amen.[6]

Alan Paton, who stirred us first as we have seldom been stirred with his tender, devastating novel *Cry, the Beloved Country,* has recalled with intimacy and surpassing beauty the years of his life with the woman

[6] Peter de Vries, *The Blood of the Lamb* (New York: New American Library, 1963), 164.

he met in 1925, later married, and who died October
23, 1967. He calls the memoirs *For You Departed*,[7]
and throughout he talks to her of his grief and his
joy, of the small and great moments of their life
together, of what was given him in her life, and above
all the impact of her death upon his perception and
appreciation of the life that was theirs, the continuing
life that is his, and the life of the children of God
that is shared by all men.

It is a part of the mystery of death, over which the
church is given a special kind of keeping, that it is
only in uncompromising acknowledgment of death
to our own, and ultimately inevitably to ourselves,
that we can comprehend and respond creatively to
death in the family of man. It is only in the midst of
the mystery of death that we know fully what it is
to be in life.

The Spanish poet Frederico García Lorca, who died
in his thirties at the instigation of the same crippled
lovers of death responsible for the demise of Unamuno, wrote an essay—the most remarkable thing
remotely of its kind that I know—entitled "Theory
and Function of the *Duende*." [8] The *duende* is the
mystery of creativity, unpredictable, indefinable, un-
harnessable. It is not, he says, the guiding angel; nor

[7] Alan Paton, *For You Departed* (New York: Charles
Scribner's Sons, 1969).
[8] Lorca, "Theory and Function of the *Duende*," in J. L.
Gill (tr. and ed.), *Lorca* (Baltimore: Penguin Books, 1960).

is it the muse. "To help us seek the *duende* there is
neither map nor discipline. All one knows is that it
burns the blood like powdered glass, that it exhausts,
that it rejects all the sweet geometry one has learned,
that it breaks with all styles. . . . The appearance of
the *duende* always presupposes a radical change of all
forms based on old structures. It gives a sensation of
freshness wholly unknown, having the quality of a
newly created rose, of miracle." [9] The *duende* presupposes a new land, a new race, a new language. It
is itself a part of the new mystery. If Paul had known
Spanish, he might have said, "Circumcision is nothing,
uncircumcision is nothing. All that matters is *duende!*"
And Lorca goes on to say: "The *duende* does not appear if it sees no possibility of death, if it does not
know that it will haunt death's house. . . . While
angel and muse are content with violin or measured
rhythm, the *duende* wounds, and in the healing of this
wound which never closes is the prodigious, the
original in the work of man." [10]

This is the old mystery that is the new mystery,
that death is *duende*. It is not simply that in the
consciousness of death we are given sensitivity to the
inexpressible wonder and mystery and beauty and
poignancy of life, but that death itself, in the de-
voted, committed, expended, *given* life, is creative.
Paton says to his departed: "I give thanks for the

[9] *Ibid.*, 129, 131.
[10] *Ibid.*, 136.

blessing of our life, for a love that persisted through vicissitudes, for a love of others that triumphed over the barriers of race and custom and was given to any person who wanted it or was in need of it, and which was so abundantly returned—good measure, pressed down, shaken together, running over. . . . *But it happens only when you give yourself with your gift.*" [11] Lorca's essay concludes with these lines: "Ladies and Gentlemen: I have raised three arches and with clumsy hands I have placed in them the muse, the angel, and the *duende*. The muse remains quiet . . . the angel may stir. [But] the *duende*—where is the *duende?* Through the empty arch comes an air of the mind that blows insistently over the heads of the dead, in search of new landscapes and unsuspected accents . . . and announcing the constant baptism of newly created things." [12]

So let me conclude these brief chapters. Somewhere in our tradition, three crosses have been raised. Two are quiet, but over and through and around the empty cross in the center comes a wind that blows insistently over the whole conspiracy of death. It is the *duende*, the wind of creativity; it is what the Old Testament calls the *ruach-Yahweh*; in the church it is the power of God in Christ, the whole conspiracy of grace in search of new landscapes and unsuspected

[11] Paton, *For You Departed*, 13.
[12] Lorca, "Theory and Function of the Duende," 139.

accents and announcing the constant baptism of newly created things.

The only thing that really counts now is new creation toward a new history—a new land, a new people,
a new language, all made possible in a new understanding of an old mystery. The insistent wind over
the heads of all the self-given dead and over our own
dying; the insistent wind from all the unceasingly
emptied crosses; the insistent wind from the one
central empty cross has blown on us all.

And we are able if we will to move toward a new
history, toward new creation. God's name be praised!

DATE DUE

F			

DEMCO 38-297